DIVINE APPOINTMENTS

How God Used One Woman to Affect Many...

An Autobiography of
Edna Adam - Simpson (nee Feuerbach)

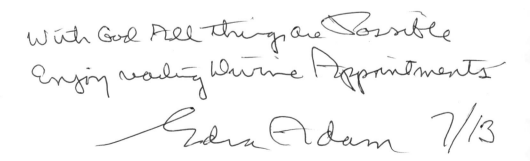

With God All things are Possible
Enjoy reading Divine Appointments
Edna Adam 7/13

Divine Appointments

Self published
Printed by Gorham Printing
Centralia, Washington USA
First Edition, First Printing
Printed in the United States of America

ISBN: 978-0-615-39548-7

Written by Edna Adam
Edited by Liz Snell, Tim Adam, Kathie Adam
Cover Design by Kathie Adam

Printing and Bindery by Gorham Printing

For copies of this book or to contact the Author
e-mail: joedna@msn.com

For my children:
Fern, Daniel, Grace, Timothy,
Ruth, Eunice, Mark, their children
and their children's children....

Foreword

Energetic – that's my Mom. She has always loved to get her hands on a good project and she has gotten her hands on a lot as you'll get to read. In my own memory, there were our family canning bees: peaches, pears, plums, cherries all colorfully lining our shelves ready to be served all winter long for dessert. Then there is the story of her getting her foot broken by our cow as she became a working Mom here in Canada; running not only a raspberry farm, but also seven children. And all this was BEFORE she and dad opened our home to drifting young people in Vancouver, B.C. She has just kept on going.

So what is the source of all her energetic youthfulness? The artesian well on the farm of my teen years might give you a bit of a picture of Mom's life. Our pond could only stay full all through our hot Victoria summers because of the water bubbling up from much deeper. Mom long ago tapped into her own well--her Lord and Savior, Jesus Christ – and it shows.

After all the changes, loss and sixty some odd moves of her life, Mom still meets life with gusto. She travels the continent with Joe still striking up conversations with strangers before she lands at our home to play games (Mexican Train, Rook or Scrabble anyone?) and fills the house with laughter. My mom only WINTERS at the Fountain of Youth spa in Niland, California, she's been young forever.

Here are Mom's adventures as they unfolded, left in print as a legacy for us all. My "never too old" mom might just inspire us all to ask, "What else awaits me?"

Enjoy!

Eunice Joy (#6)

Reader's Note

Being asked by an author to read for them is a matter of high honor and trust. However, like any authentic relationship it is entered into with a good measure of caution and trepidation.

Lucky for us all, Edna's story was ripe and ready to be told.

Through the entire process, Edna generously allowed me the freedom to be honest and frank in all my comments and suggestions.

Most important and happily for me, she accepted the most candid criticisms with grace and responded with energy. In return, she delivered to us this rich and wonder-filled story.

There are, no doubt, many lapses and untold adventures in Edna's story. Anyone with a life as full as Edna's has been cannot be expected to write everything down! It is my hope that you will be able to satisfy your questions and curiosities regarding Edna's life and experiences in conversations with her for years to come.

Sue Ament
Fountain of Youth 2010

CONTENTS

Acknowledgements

Many people have asked what inspired me to write my story. Over the years my family has told me, "Mom you should write your story." I would reply, "Me with a grade four education! How is that possible?" They would reply, "All you have to do is talk into a tape recorder and we will transcribe it and make a book." Sounds simple, too good to be true. Many years have gone by and I often thought, perhaps someday I would tell my story.

At age 76 I bought a computer, now I was ready to write my story. I soon realized that I needed to type and tell the computer what to write. I even bought some software, 'How to write my story'. I learned the hard way, persevering and in slow motion. I often scolded and yelled at the computer.

My friend Margaret Tomita saw my dilemma and offered to type for me. I wrote in long hand and she kept typing and correcting all my mistakes.

One day my neighbour Sue came over and I shared my struggles with her. She is a writer and offered to be my reader. I had no idea what that meant, but I handed her a couple of pages to take home and read. The next day she brought them back all in red markings. She told me the content was interesting but the grammar and spelling left much to be desired. I told Joe that I did not want her to read any more of my writing. Sue encouraged me and promised to use green ink instead of red. She continued to do the reading and Margaret continued to type. I also had some of my family do typing.

Grace, Eunice and Daniel all typed a good amount for me. Tim and Kathie helped me edit and format many times as I kept inserting and would mix up the formatting again. All my children read portions of it for me and made comments.

With all the help I received, I was able to finally get it all on the computer. Now I was ready for my family to do the rest, put it all together into a book like they had promised a long time ago.

My son Daniel and Kathie came to visit at the spa. I told him that I had all the material on the computer and asked him to put it all together. He is an Architect and would have had no problems. Well to my disappointment he said, "Mom I can't do it for you. You need a focus or theme for the book, and then work from there." We brained stormed and I couldn't think of a focus. Nothing popped into my head.

Then I said, "I always wanted to attend my own funeral."

Like a light, Daniel said, "That's it!" Then he excused himself and went to join Kathie for a siesta. I took a pen and paper and started to write about attending my own funeral. The inspiration just flowed. I couldn't stop writing. When Daniel and Kathie came back into the room I read what I had written. Kathie with great excitement said, "That is awesome!"

From then on everything came together. My granddaughter Liz Snell, who is taking writing at University, offered to help with the editing and to provide professional advice. She came and spent 3 weeks with me ironing out details.

Kathie came up with the title and offered to prepare it for the printers, doing all the hard work inserting pictures and formatting. Family members and friends sent contributions. Joe patiently and without complaining spent much of his time sitting on the deck watching the birds and flowers, while I worked inside expressing my frustrations at the computer. This was truly a labour of love on everyone's behalf and I thank you all.

I would especially like to acknowledge Joe for his patience with me during the many, many hours of writing and talking about my story.

Some people have asked if it is a true story. My reply is, "As I remember it. Others may remember some details differently."

My prayer is that you will enjoy reading it and perhaps be inspired to trust God more in His faithfulness.

Introduction

I am getting old and I am living on borrowed time. I had hoped to finish writing my story by the time I had reached my 80th birthday but I kept putting it off thinking I had plenty of time. Now I am over 85 and my mind is not as sharp and my eyesight is failing but I am determined to write my story before I die.

Lately, I have been thinking a lot about dying and my funeral. Growing up my family didn't talk much about death or dying but the Bible speaks a lot about death. Ps. 23; 'Even though I walk through the valley of the shadow of death, I will fear no evil, for you are with me.' 'If death is a shadow, then it can't hurt us.' John 5:24; 'He has crossed over from death to life.' 1Cor. 15:54; 'Death has been swallowed up in victory.' Rev. 2:10; 'Be faithful, even to the point of death and I will give you the crown of life.'

Rev. 21:4 says that in Heaven there will be no more death and Jn. 14 says that Jesus is preparing a Mansion for us in Heaven. I look forward to taking possession of mine real soon.

It wasn't until this dream that it all came together...

Chapter 1
The Dream

Last night I dreamed I attended my own funeral and as the funeral progressed my whole life flashed before my eyes.

When I arrived at the funeral I heard them singing one of my favourite hymns,

Just a Closer Walk with Thee
Grant it Jesus is my plea
Daily walking close to Thee
Let it be dear Lord, let it be

I sat down in the very front row and meditated on the hymn. Yes, this is my prayer - to have a closer walk with Jesus. I hope this is also the prayer of my family.

Looking around, there sure were lots of people. Many of them I did not recognize. I wondered why they had all come to my funeral. I looked at my coffin. It was simple but nice. I could see my body lying dressed in my navy blue suit and white blouse. I noticed a very large fork lying beside me in the coffin. At first I wondered what the meaning of the fork could be but then I remembered a story I told my kids.

It was about an old lady who had requested a fork be placed in her coffin. She was asked why she wanted a fork. Her explanation was that, as a child her mother always reminded them to keep their fork after the main dish because the best was yet to come - dessert. I went on to tell them that her best was waiting for her in Heaven so she needed a fork. I was glad my children remembered that story.

There were lots of my favourite flowers on and around the coffin – roses, carnations and sweet peas. I was pleased that my family had remembered how much I loved flowers.

I was glad to see Joe sitting in the front row with my family. They all love him and he has been a great blessing to my family

I saw some of my grandchildren with video cameras. I always wanted my funeral on video for future generations to see. There were pictures of past family reunions displayed all around the hall and a slide show could be viewed on one side of the room. Family reunions were always very important to our family.

It was quiet for a few moments, then my son Daniel stood up. He walked slowly to the front and looked down at the coffin. He stood there for a while lost in his thoughts and when he finally turned around it was obvious that he was deeply moved, tears spilled from his eyes but his face had a large smile.

I am Edna's eldest son," he began softly. *"Some of you have known her as a friend, as a bocce ball competitor or a scrabble partner. To all of you who have shared her life here at the Fountain of Youth, thank you for providing friendship and companionship to my mother in her old age. Others may have heard her tell stories of a childhood on a prairie homestead, doing what was necessary to survive the winters, the chores, the hard times. Although the journey of her life took her to many countries, the values learned on a farm remained important to her; to work hard, to share what you have with others, to be modest, to be frugal with money, to be resourceful, to cook what you have, to be a good neighbor, that chores need to get done no matter how you feel, that even a tom-boy longs to be understood and loved, that sometimes you have to fight for what matters to you, that teachers would rather have respect than a black eye.*

Most of you know of her faith and her desire to serve God, which led Edna to encounters with many remarkable people around the world, some of whom are here today. You know her as a woman of courage and adventure and faith. She did not hide her spiritual lamp under the proverbial bushel. She believed a person was never 'too old'.

These are memories that you expect to hear at a memorial service and I hope more of you will tell stories from your own experiences with my mother.

However, only my brothers and sisters knew Edna as a mother. She birthed us, nursed us, fed us baby food and changed our diapers. You don't get to choose your parents or your children, but you do choose how you spend your time with them. In the last few years my mother phoned me weekly and made an effort to connect with her grandchildren. I will miss that.

I remember an incident from when we lived in Ootacamund, South India. It was late afternoon and my mother was driving our old Vanguard up the hill. At one point she could not see the road because of where the sun was but she managed to slow down and safely pull over to the shoulder. She was alarmed to realize that in the emergency she had instinctively resorted to her oldest driving habits and had been driving on the wrong side of the road for India. It seems that no matter what you learn later in life, what you learned and experienced when you were young stays with you.

Growing up on a farm my mom had learned to can fruit and vegetables, to butcher animals and to bake bread. In our family, with so many kids, we would set up an assembly line and fill hundreds of canning jars with pickles, pears, peaches, cherries, plums and applesauce. Those colorful jars lined the pantry shelves and we always seemed to have a stock of preserves. I remember how we sometimes cut up and wrapped large animals or made sausage. Her German heritage showed in her love of baking; bread, cinnamon buns, strudel, doughnuts, pies, cakes, even dumplings in the stew.

In India she discovered how to cook with exotic spices — some of you have enjoyed her wonderful pilau. She also learned that you need a pressure cooker to prepare meat from water buffalo that are too old to work in the fields anymore.

Hospitality was important to my parents and I can remember how we regularly shared our dining table with others. Sometimes another family would be invited after church for Sunday dinner, or sometimes the youth group from church would be fed — I met my wife that way! My parents ran a guest house in South India called Farley, which was like a Bed and Breakfast retreat for exhausted missionaries who needed to be refreshed in body and spirit. In Vancouver they opened up their home to transient young people. Some had been involved with the drug culture, others were deciding what to do with their lives. All of them were fed at our hospitality table. Money was limited, but a resourceful farm girl can make a tasty roast out of a baloney roll. I love that quality in my mom; she was generous even when she didn't have a lot to share.

In keeping with that spirit of hospitality I would like to invite each of you to the Hall next door to share some food and to meet the family. I think mom would have liked that very much, from what I fondly remember of her hospitality and also from the fork you may have noticed in her hand.

I sat there and wept, I was so proud to be his mother. I bowed my head and said a prayer. Then my sister-in-law appeared at the microphone.

"My name is Leona Hehr. Edna was married to my brother Alfred. I remember Edna telling Bible stories to the children who sat wide-eyed and attentive as these stories came alive as only Edna could tell them. Edna graciously opened her home in Kelowna to me, for five months. I will always remember and appreciate her encouraging words and her prayers during that time when I so desperately needed them.

"I also remember Edna making it her mission, to share with the people on the streets and in the parks in Kelowna. She never missed an opportunity to share her testimony."

And then another sister-in law spoke.

"My name is Myrtle Adam. Edna is my sister in law. One memory that has stayed with me is Edna's faithfulness in having devotions each day with her children. Another memory that lingers happened one day when Edna was out. We had chicken for dinner and Alfred put aside a choice piece for her. It was a lesson in unselfishness for me.

"Through the years we have enjoyed fellowship in the raspberry patch, Cultus Lake and at family reunions. When Alfred and Edna lived in their daughter Grace's basement we made frequent trips from Kamloops to visit. Our main pastime was playing different versions of Rook. One weekend we had such an enjoyable time that the next Saturday, on the spur of the moment, we decided to drive to Vancouver again. When we arrived I opened the door and called "the kids are here again!"

"Another enjoyable time was Edna's 80th birthday celebration. It was so much fun we wished we could have a repeat every year.

"We deeply cherish these memories and are happy that her children are continuing this tradition."

Hearing everyone speak brought back so many memories my mind wandered into the past.

Chapter 2
My Childhood

My mother was born in the Ukraine in 1882. Her maiden name was Matilda Schoenfeld. At 16 she married John Feuerbach. In the late 1800s, they left their farm and migrated to Canada with two children. We never asked my mother why they left, but we overheard the neighbors and her share gruesome stories of the brutalities the local soldiers committed against the German Ukrainian civilians. She never told us about the Ukraine, so all we knew came from the snatches we heard her tell the neighbors.

Mom and Helen

From the Ukraine, my parents arrived in Montreal and took the train to Winnipeg. My father got a job working on the railroad and my mother worked in the hospital as a cleaning lady. She told us how she had to wear white gloves and keep everything spotless.

While in Winnipeg, they heard that the government was encouraging immigrants to claim land north of Winnipeg. They could buy a one-quarter section (160 acres) for ten dollars. So my family left the city and moved out to Moosehorn, Manitoba. They rented a place while they waited to get their land from the Hudson Bay Company, which represented the Government. When they got their land, they had to build a house to live in and barns for the animals. The neighbors rallied to help the newcomers. The quarter section that they bought was covered in trees, mostly black poplars. When the land was cleared of poplars, they went out to the bush to chop down spruce, which the lumber mill then cut into rough boards. Our neighbor Mr. Bittner squared and smoothed the lumber off with an axe. Everyone worked to raise the frames and cover the roofs of the house and barns with sod.

The land then had to be cleared to plant a garden and sow a crop of wheat and oats. They discovered that it was full of stones, which had to be removed by hand. They also had to dig a well for water. In the meantime they carried the water from a neighbor's well half a mile away. Digging our well was an expensive project as it was over forty feet deep. Fortunately, it provided plenty of water.

After my parents arrived in Moosehorn, they had eight more children. I had eight brothers; William, Arthur, Manuel, Henry, Roy, Leo, Edward and Leonard and three sisters: Emma, Helena and Elsie. I was the last of the twelve children. On October 6, 1924, in the middle of a great storm, which took the roof off our house, I was born, weighing 13 pounds. My parents named me Edna Ernestina but I was usually called Tina as a child. Most of my brothers and sisters had left home before I was old enough to know them so I remember very little about the older ones.

When I was six months old, my father left to find work in BC. My mother never saw him again. I'm amazed how she managed to work the farm and raise such a large family alone. To me, she was like the 'Virtuous Woman' in Proverbs 31, which states:

"She buys wool and willingly works with her hands. She rises while it is yet night and provides food for her household. She stretches out her hands to the distaff and her hand holds the spindle. She is not afraid of the snow for she clothes her family with homemade clothes. She makes woollen garments and sells them. She watches over the ways of her household and does not eat the bread of idleness. Her children rise up and call her blessed."

My mother had all of these good qualities. She could make delicious meals out of anything and turn old clothes into new ones. She knitted and sewed and I would often hear the hum of her spinning wheel until two or three in the morning. She was strong and bold, willing to try anything. The only thing she was afraid of was the dark and staying home alone. These fears were ones I inherited from her and kept for many years. One of us would always have to stay home with her.

Sometimes we all went to a dance and she would go with us, keeping a careful eye on our behavior. She got a German Bible from a Jehovah's Witness traveling salesman and used to read it quite often, but never to us. We went to church only at Easter and Christmas or for other special occasions.

My mother took control of everything; she was always in charge. A plump, short, strong woman, she always wore her hair up in a bun, often covered by a black beret. She always spoke to us in German, but then everyone in Moosehorn did. Even the church services were in German.

One time she needed to discipline Eddy, who was about 18 and a strong young man. She took a big stick to him and he grabbed hold of the other end. She was so angry he got double what he deserved. That was the last time Eddy tried to mess with Mother. Mother knew how to take charge, but she wasn't always fair. Fairness is a big issue for me; I'm still learning that life isn't always fair.

One day in the deep winter, Leonard, Mother and I went to visit our neighbors, the Galls, who lived a mile and a half away. Spring, summer and fall were always busy seasons, but in winter there was less work to be done and more time to visit, although the weather was harsh and kept us mostly indoors. We knew everyone around and we would all stop by each other's places without an invitation. In the light of the kerosene lamp, we gathered to play simple games such as "Button, Button, who's got the Button" and "Milchan." That day, when it was time to leave, Leonard led Dandy our chestnut horse from the barn and hitched him up to the sleigh in the dark. Dandy shook his mane and stamped his feet against the frozen ground, ready to go home. Mother wrapped me in thick wool blankets and put heated rocks under my feet. I was thinking of the chores still left to do at home before it got too cold, but at least Leonard would have to help me. I settled deeper under the blankets.

Coming up beside me, Leonard handed me the reins. "I'm going to stay a little longer."

I sat up with a start. "What?" All evening I had watched Leonard watching Herta. She was the oldest of the three Gall sisters. I knew very well why he wanted to stay.

"Mother . . . " I pled.

"That's alright, Tina, I said he could stay." I cracked the reins sharply and glared as we moved away from the house.

"That's not fair! Now I have to do all the chores by myself and I am only 14!"

My hands ached with cold as I held onto the reins. I would have to go out to the barn to do all the chores by myself in the dark. Beside me, Mother began coughing. Although she was strong, she was often sick with pleurisy and other illnesses. Dandy knew where he was going and soon we were back at home. Mother was too weak to help with the chores, so I lit the lamp and helped her to bed. I then went out into the dark, cold night.

Picking up the axe, I carried it over to the cow trough and swung it down breaking the ice so the cows and horses could drink the water underneath. I boiled a kettle and carried the hot water out to the pump, pouring it over the handle to thaw it. Up and down I pumped the squeaking handle, pulling up more water for the thirsty animals. When they had finished drinking, the cows and horses stood by the back door of the barn ready to rush in as soon as I opened the door. I shooed them apart watching that they didn't crush each other, then tied them all up and pitched hay into the manger to feed them. I carried in water for the pigs, chickens and geese. Then I began to milk the cows. My hands were stiff with cold and frustration. I could just imagine Leonard sitting cozily back at the Galls, talking to Herta and her sisters and warming his feet by the fire.

"Tina!" The barn door opened and two children stepped inside the lantern's glow. They were Walter and Edna Middlestead, the neighbor children from half a mile away. They were from a large, poor family and often stopped by to visit. Walter, who was my age, seemed particularly fond of me. He came over to me and asked, "Where's Lowney?"

"He got to stay at the Galls and I have to do all the chores by myself," I complained.

"Well... we can help you," he said. We finished milking the cows together. Then the three of us carried the milk into the pump house and poured it into the separator. The handle had to be turned at just the right speed to get the right consistency, until the cream and milk had separated. Then we took all the separator pieces into the house and washed them in warm water. We hauled loads of wood from the shed into the house to keep the fire going all night. While Mother slept in bed, we sat in the kitchen playing poker for a nickel until Walter and Edna had to leave. I took the lamp into the bedroom and went in to sit with Mother.

"Why did Leonard get to stay with the Galls?" I asked. "It was not really fair that he got to stay." She looked up at me, the lamp shining on her lined face.

"Oh Tina, don't complain. Let your brother have a little fun at the Galls. It is only for awhile." I lay down on my bed and stared at the wall until I fell asleep.

Elsie, Walter my nephew & Me

Elsie was the only sister at home with me. She was considered the delicate one so she stayed inside and did the housework while I became a feisty tomboy. I was always outside playing and working with my brothers rather than doing housework with her.

I didn't like school and found learning very hard. It didn't help that school wasn't a priority in my family. Some of my older brothers and sisters didn't attend at all and couldn't read or write. I guess I was privileged to attend school, but I missed many days of classes. In summer there was too much work; in winter it was too cold. The government would send us packages of winter clothes but nothing ever matched. We would get two right-hand mitts or two boots for left feet and coats that were too small. We certainly couldn't go to school like that so as a result I had a hard time keeping up with the

lessons. It was far from town and five kilometres from home.

Bayton School was a white, one room schoolhouse, built on land donated from the Harvard's farm. In the back of the classroom stood a huge potbelly stove where we kept ourselves warm and roasted potatoes that we brought from home to have for our lunch.

In winter I came to school pulled on a little homemade sleigh by one or two strong dogs. Behind the school there was a barn for horses and dogs. During lunch hour the boys and I would encourage the dogs to fight in the barn. We untied them from their corners and brought them together. They growled and snapped, biting each other until they bled. The girls covered their eyes and ran away, but I stayed with the boys, egging on the dogs.

Mr. Luckow, our teacher, lived in the little cottage behind the school. He was Jewish, tall and skinny with dark hair. He was the only teacher we had for all eight grades so he didn't have time to give individual help. I don't remember ever passing a test except when I copied from Ella. She was my best friend at school and sat beside me. Ella was good at school but I wasn't interested in learning.

It was hard work to control kids in a rural school so in those days the school supplied the teachers with a strap made from old car tire rubber. I was always in the line up of children waiting to be punished.

"Hold out your hand," Mr. Luckow would tell us sternly. The other students would put out a trembling hand and look down at the floor, some of them crying even before he brought the strap down. When he got to me, he always did his best to sound intimidating. As he brought the strap down I quickly pulled my hand away. The strap hit his leg with a sharp crack and we all laughed as our teacher winced in anger and pain.

Once, as Mr. Luckow bent over a desk helping one of the youngest students sound out a word, I stretched an elastic band and shot it at him, as I often did. This time, it hit him straight on the nose. Mr. Luckow wheeled around. "Who shot that elastic?" The students sat in their seats, eyes wide. I tried to look as innocent as the rest, but I knew I was his primary suspect. "Alright, you can all just sit there until you decide to tell me who did it."

He stomped out of the classroom and into his little cottage. Before long, the students were running around the room laughing and throwing things. The door opened again and Mr. Luckow walked stiffly up to the front of the room. "Well, if you don't want to listen to me, I challenge you to a wrestling match. Who will accept?"

I eagerly put up my hand, along with three boys and one other girl. We followed Mr. Luckow outside grinning at each other. I wasn't scared; to me, everything was a challenge. "Everyone make a circle," Mr. Luckow said and the students spread out around us.

All the fighters got in the middle of the circle and Mr. Luckow told us the rules. If anyone fell they would be disqualified. We all rushed at Mr. Luckow and grappled with him. The students yelled our names. They were clearly on the side of their classmates. It wasn't long before Mr. Luckow had gotten down the two boys and the other girl. Now I was the only one left. Taller than all the rest, I dodged and swung at him. Try as he might to catch me, I remained standing. He lunged towards me, but I ducked. My fist flew at his face and he was soon on the ground, bent over in the dust, clutching at his left eye.

"Everybody in the schoolroom!" he shouted. He walked back to the cottage and then sent for me. The skin around his eye was beginning to turn purple. Frowning, he stood looking down at me and said, "Tina, you must wash my dishes every day for a week." So all that week, I scrubbed his dishes after school. But as Mr. Luckow stood in front of the class, his black eye was a reminder to everyone that Tina the tomboy had beaten the teacher 'real good.'

By the time I was 14, I was legally allowed to leave school. This was fine by me and probably by Mr. Luckow too! Grade four was the farthest I got and was the last education I had for many years.

I loved a challenge, not just at school, but wherever I was. I rode horses bareback and sometimes got thrown off. Sometimes I would drive the horses too fast. Once in the winter I was driving my mother into town to go shopping. Dandy was a racer and loved to go fast; rather than a jolting gallop, he had a long, smooth stride. We always had to hold him back when driving. This time, I decided to let him go. I sat up in the sleigh, feeling the wind sting my face, grinning as he went faster and faster.

"Tina!" my mother yelled from beside me. Suddenly, I could feel the sleigh tipping. Pulling hard on the reigns, I screamed as the sleigh tilted over. When we stopped, I couldn't see Mother.

"Mother!" I shouted. I heard muffled sounds from the side of the road. Looking over, I could see my mother struggling out of one of the high snow banks lining the road. I rushed to help her up. She made sure we drove very slowly the rest of the way to town.

My nephews Walter and Albert Wensel

Horses always held a special interest for me. We bought an old horse named Barney from Mr. Scholtz, a drunkard. Barney was so frail he looked like he could hardly run, but Mr. Scholtz would shout a German command, "Schultz fah!" and Barney would take off and go like crazy. We also bought a grey Appaloosa mare named Flossie. She was a beautiful horse but sometimes she bit us. To breed her we called a man with a stallion to come over. He fed the stallion raw eggs because it made him more interested in mating. Flossie gave us two colts, which I had to break. Sometimes I would hook one up to the carriage and Mother would come out of the house and say, "What? Are we going to go to town with that wild horse?"

When I'd jump on the horses in the meadow without a bridle it was very difficult to stay on, but it was even harder to ride a cow. In the spring when all the sloughs were full, we'd jump on a calf or cow and try to ride across the flooded ditches but we'd usually end up being dumped off into the water.

I was always doing daring things. One day I was chased by a ferocious bull while walking through a pasture on the way to school. Luckily I managed to escape over the fence.

Other funny things happened to me on the way to school. Once I was walking along the road when a group of boys from school came along. "Dare you to jump over the ditch," they said. The roadside ditch was wide, but I had to take the challenge. I found a long stick and planted it in the middle of the ditch, but when I put my weight on it to swing myself over, I fell right into the middle of it. I clambered out thoroughly soaked, the boys laughing at me. As I continued on to school, my crepe dress began to dry, but it kept getting shorter. By the time I got to school, it was way above my knees. I didn't want to go inside the schoolhouse, but I knew I'd already get in enough trouble from my mother for shrinking my dress. I walked in and put my books on my desk, pretending that nothing was wrong, but everyone began to laugh. They asked, "Whatever happened to you?" I laughed as if I didn't care. "Some bullies dared me to jump over a ditch. I almost got over." I sat at my desk trying to pull my dress down over my knees, just waiting for the day to be over.

I had plenty of embarrassing moments. One Sunday afternoon my friend and I were visiting one of our neighbors. Bored of the adult conversation, we went out to the barn to play hide-and-seek, ducking behind stalls and climbing up into the hayloft. We were wearing our Sunday best dresses but were sure we could keep them clean.

"Can't catch me!" I yelled, running as hard as I could to touch home base. Halfway there, I slipped. I reached out to protect my dress and myself but it was too late – I fell flat on my face into a juicy, freshly made cow patty. My friend looked at me in shock.

"Oh, Tina! What are you going to do now?"

"I don't know." My Sunday dress was a mess. I was scared to death of what Mother would do when I arrived home.

My friend led me out of the barn to the horse trough. "Let's try to wash it off," she said. She scrubbed at the front of my dress, but the brown stain only got spread around. Now I was not only dirty but soaking wet. We waited until the dress was dry before going inside. My mother took one look at my dress and shook her head and when we got home, she marched me straight to the woodshed for a thrashing.

At Halloween there were no costumes or trick-or-treating, but this was the time of year when our creative juices really flowed. One of our favorite tricks was to move our neighbor's outhouses. At night in the dark when they went to the outhouse they would fall into the filthy hole. This was a dirty trick and those who'd fallen prey to it would get very angry and arm themselves with their shotguns. But we had no fear. The more they threatened the more fun we had.

Another favorite Halloween trick was to exchange the wagon wheels by placing the big ones in the front and the smaller ones at the back. Sometimes we would pull the wagons to the top of the haystack. The next morning there were angry farmers swearing, determined to catch and punish us. But they never could.

I wasn't as happy when tricks were played on me, however. One day in the spring Ella came up to me holding something in her hand. She said, "Open your mouth and close your eyes. I'll give you something to make you wise." I closed my eyes and opened my mouth, thinking it would be a candy. Feeling something smooth on my tongue, I closed my mouth. I bit through something crunchy and then I felt gritty ooze. Gagging in horror, I spit it out in a hurry. It was an almost-hatched bird's egg! I couldn't believe Ella had played such a nasty trick on me. I think that was the end of our friendship for a good long while.

Ella wasn't the only friend who gave me trouble. In the wintertime I kept a trap line. I set a circle of snares out on rabbit trails and near stone piles where weasels lived. One day I went out to check the traps and found a black and white creature with a bushy tail, dead. "I caught a skunk!" I told all my friends.

"Dare you to skin it," they said. I was the only one who would try something like that, but I was determined to prove I could do it and sell the hide. I got my knife and began peeling the skin off the skunk. It was easy, just like skinning a rabbit. Then suddenly there was a terrible stench – I'd hit the scent gland with my knife. I gagged on the smell; it was awful. When I tried to go inside, Mother said, "You're not going to come in smelling like that."

It was winter, however, and I couldn't very well stay locked outside. I scrubbed myself with lye soap as well as I could, but the smell stayed on. Everyone in the house avoided me. I didn't speak to my friends who had dared me to skin the skunk for at least a week, but then, they probably didn't want to come near me either. Never again did I want a skunk in my traps.

My brother Roy was a better trapper than I was and spent most of his life in the bush. When he came home for a visit, he would share stories about his adventures. One time he was surrounded by a pack of timber wolves. Wolves travel in packs of 10 to 15. Roy knew he didn't have enough bullets to shoot them all. The wolves were all around him, their eyes glinting as they closed in for the attack. In desperation he cried out to God for help. He wasn't a religious man, but God heard his cry. Suddenly the wolves turned and ran away.

Once he brought home a new revolver, proudly showing it to everyone. The only kind of gun I'd used on the farm was a 22 rifle. I'd never seen a revolver and admired it very much.

"Can I hold it? Please?" I asked.

"Be careful," he said, handing it to me. I admired the shining metal and glossy wood. Lifting it up and pointing it at my brother Mac's head, I put my finger on the trigger and was about to click it back.

"Check to see if it's empty!" Roy yelled. I hadn't even thought to check. Sure enough, when I opened it up, there was a bullet in the revolver. I came so close to shooting my own brother! I never touched that revolver again. God spared me from a disaster.

Roy stayed home one summer to help us with the haying. He was fun to work with and I helped him build his own canoe. There were no lakes near our place but he needed it for his trapping expeditions. He was quite a craftsman. He soaked the lumber and bent it into shape, covered it with waterproof material, then painted it deep green. When it was finally finished, it looked like a professional job. We were so proud of ourselves and I was glad he spent that summer at home.

During the Depression times got tough and people did whatever they could to earn extra money. Many of the farmers made moonshine and we joined them. In the Bible Joshua made the sun stand still, but my mother made the moon shine. She had a good recipe and made the best moonshine in the neighborhood. People came from miles away to buy it but I hated everything about the moonshine business.

Since making moonshine was illegal, we had to hide it in various secret places. The outhouse was a great place and we made a secret space inside it to conceal the moonshine. We also hid it in rock piles and in the haystack. We had a secret trapdoor in the ceiling of a cow stall in the middle of the barn. It led to a space between the bales of hay, where we kept the barrels of rye, wheat and sugar as they fermented.

At night, we would take the brew out through the trapdoor and heat it over a steady fire. In the winter, it would take about three weeks for the brine to clear, which was how we knew when it was finished brewing. In the summer, it took only about a week. In the summer we set up the still in the pasture, but in the winter we moved our operations into the chicken coop. It was my job to sit in the coop all night poking the fire, which was a dangerous business. Sometimes when I put too much wood on the fire, the wooden plug would blow out of the boiler and the hot brew would spray everywhere. Not a drop would be left. I could easily have been badly scalded.

The chickens liked to eat the leftover grain after the brew had been extracted, but when they ate too much we'd find them stumbling around drunk. It wasn't just the chickens. Once when we went to bring the cows in for the night, we found them lying by the moonshine barrels we'd hid in the pasture. They had got into the moonshine and drank so much they were bloated and nearly dead. The neighbor came and poked some holes in their stomachs and none of them died. I guess the cows learned their lesson, because they never got drunk again.

I also had to deliver the moonshine to customers in five-gallon cream cans by dog sled. Sometimes a rabbit would run across the road and the dogs would take after it. The cream cans would fly off the sled and roll away. I had to retrieve the dogs, load the cans back on the sled and continue the eleven-mile journey to the customers. Sometimes Leonard and I would sell several bottles of moonshine and split the money we earned between us, without telling Mother.

The worst part of the business was the drunks. Sometimes they would arrive in the middle of the day. When Mother refused to sell them moonshine, they would get very angry. Many times they would come in the middle of the night, which was worst in the winter. Mother yelled at them, "Come back when you're sober!"

"We'll break down your door!" they replied. "Tina, open the door," Mother said wearily. So I got up out of bed, shivering with cold and fear. Opening the door, I stepped back quickly as they forced their way in, laughing and shouting, leering in my face. Then I had to go outside to get the moonshine. I pulled on a jacket over my nightgown and went out into temperatures that could be below forty degrees, with snow piled high and blowing around me. As I lugged the bottles out from one of our hiding spots, I hunched my shoulders against the cold and hoped the drunks would leave quickly. When it came to threats, there was no choice but to give them what they wanted. We knew they wouldn't hesitate to break down the door and force us out.

One day when I arrived home, I could hear Mother screaming. Following the sound of her cries, I found her tied up to the wagon. She looked exhausted and angry. I ran to help untie her. "Mother! What happened?" "The drunks came," she said. "They took all our moonshine." Sure enough, all the hidden stashes were gone and I had to work even harder to make sure the next batch brewed properly.

Despite these troubles, few women could handle drunks like Mother could. Often, we had dances in the granary to get more moonshine customers. Someone played the fiddle while everyone danced and drank and drank some more. One time a vicious fight broke out. As the blows became more and more fierce, I climbed on top of the tables for safety. Then my mother was in the middle of the mess, screaming at the guests. She grabbed two men and knocked their heads together as hard as she could, then dragged them into the bedroom and locked the door. After that, things settled down.

One winter day we saw a sleigh racing up to our house, carrying three red-coated men.

"The Mounties!" One of the Mounties marched us into the house and guarded the door while the other two searched the farm. Picking up a pitchfork they jabbed it into the hay. There was a sharp sound. Pulling the hay aside, they quickly uncovered the fresh batch of moonshine we'd just made. "Now bring us the still," they said.

I went out to the chicken coop and brought in all the pieces of the still. I wanted to throw them at the jugs of moonshine and break the evidence, but I was too scared of what the Mounties might do. They fined us $50. With the loss of the $50, the moonshine and the still, I had to shoot rabbits and trap weasels to make more money. Despite the risk, we kept right on making moonshine. One day a cattle buyer came to our place. We didn't know he was in cahoots with the Mounties so we sold him some booze. He took it straight back to them. They came to our place again and found another hidden stash. This time we were fined a hundred dollars. I had to trap more rabbits and weasels.

"Next time it'll be jail, ma'am," they warned my mother.

The threat from the Mounties came to a sudden end with the beginning of World War II. With sugar rationed, we couldn't make moonshine anymore. I was very happy that there was no more sitting in the chicken coop poking the fire and watching the jars fill up with moonshine, no more fines to pay and no more drunks coming to our house.

Life on the farm was mostly hard work but every year on July 1st we got to go to town for the Dominion Day celebrations. First we had to get our chores done. We rushed around the farm feeding animals, milking cows, pumping water and tending to the garden.

Then we hitched Dandy and Flossie up to the wagon and Mother, Elsie, Leonard and I rode into town. The whole town had come out. There was a big picnic, sack races, three-legged races and baseball games. During the year, the kids played baseball with a homemade bat and a ball of twine covered in a cut-up old glove, but on Dominion Day they held big baseball competitions with proper equipment.

On these holidays Mother handed each of us a quarter to spend. I would look around at all the vendors, holding my quarter tightly in my hand. The food was usually too much to resist and before long I bought ice cream, cold lemonade and a hot dog. With the leftover nickel, I picked out some candy for later.

As we got older, there were also Saturday night dances to attend. Elsie and I knew Mother could be very strict so we never wanted to ask her if we could go in case she refused. We made secret plans to get ready anyways. We would go out behind the haystack to do each other's hair in rags so it would curl. If Mother said we couldn't go to the dance it was all for nothing. When we did get to go, Elsie was the popular one and all the boys would ask her to dance. I didn't have much rhythm so I wasn't a very good dancer, but Walter Middlestead would ask me to dance. He was as unpopular with girls as I was with boys so we usually ended up together. Despite being often left out the dances they were always great fun.

By the time I was eighteen, Mother's health was failing and she became very ill. She had often been sick but, even after a night wracked with coughing, she would tie a hot water bottle around her head and keep working, tending the carrots and potatoes, picking all the outside leaves off the beets and carrying them the half-mile back home for the cattle. In the winter, she would come home from cutting the cordwood, with her feet frozen and we would try to get the circulation back into her legs by rubbing them with snow so they wouldn't swell and turn black. Although she worked so hard, unlike me, she never complained. Once when she was lying ill in bed I complained to her, "Mother, it's not fair. I have to do so many chores. I'm the youngest and everyone always forgets about me. Even when I was a baby, they forgot to give me my bottle. They even let me fall out of the high chair and break my nose."

She looked at me with a strange expression on her face and said; "Now my child Tina knows she has a mother." I never knew what she meant, but those words always haunted me.

At last her great strength failed and she could no longer get out of bed. I was the only one left at home to take care of her and the farm. I was at a loss to know how to care for her, since I had never learned to cook or do housework. Mother knew she was dying so she asked me to call the Lutheran pastor to give her communion. I rode my bike the six miles to town to get him. There was no doctor in our small town, but as she grew weaker and weaker, I knew I needed help. Once again, I biked into town and made arrangements for a nurse to come and see Mother. The nurse did what she could but Mother became worse and eventually lost consciousness. By this time, Leonard had arrived to be with us.

On Mother's Day, I heard three knocks on the door leading upstairs. That same day one of our neighbors heard three knocks on her sewing machine. The Germans believed that this was a sign of imminent death. I had never been near a dying person, so I was glad when Mr. and Mrs. Middlestead came over to watch with us. Mother lingered on until finally, at about 11 o'clock at night, she took her last breath and was gone. Mrs. Middlestead closed her eyes then left to go home.

Leonard and I had never been through a death before and had no idea what to do. The next morning I got up to get some milk from the veranda. When I passed the bedroom, I could see a bit of blood coming from the corner of Mother's mouth and it scared me to see her like that. Feeling terrible because we didn't know what to do, we closed the door and stayed out of the room. It was awful having a dead body in the house. We waited there three days, with Mother's body in the bedroom, until our neighbor, Mrs. Gall arrived to check on us.

"Where's your mother?" she asked.

"In the bedroom," I said. Mrs. Gall opened the bedroom door and went in. A terrible smell came out of the room. When she lifted the blankets off the body, the smell became even worse. The body was decomposing. Mrs. Gall looked at Leonard and me.

"Why didn't you do anything with her?"

"We didn't know what to do," we said, feeling sick.

Mrs. Gall took all the bedding out of the room and we built a big bonfire to burn it. Then she bathed and perfumed Mother's body. The next day, Helen and her husband Julius came with the coffin and helped us make arrangements for the funeral.

The day of the funeral was rainy and cold. The service was held at the Lutheran church in Bayton. Many people came, including all my brothers and sisters except Elsie, who had just had a baby. My mother was buried in the cemetery in Moosehorn. Tough tomboy that I was, I didn't even cry at her funeral.

She was only 61 years old when she died and I was eighteen at the time. I had never really had a chance to know who she was because she never talked about her feelings or her past. I never even knew if she had brothers or sisters.

From left to right: Julius Wensel, Walter Wensel, Lenord Rapke, Helen Wensel, Lenord Edna, Eddie Feuerbach, Edith Wensel, Henry Feuerbach, baby Ron Feuerbach, Alma Feuerbach

My Family in Moosehorn, Manitoba 1940, standing in front of Julius' car, from left to right: Walter Wensel (nephew),Mother (Matilda Firebach), Me, Elsie, Helen, Julius, Leonard

From left to right, My oldest sister Emma and her two daughters: Lillian Fredrick, Edna Fredrick, Emma Fredrick, Children are Emma's grandkids

Chapter 3
A Promise to God

Shortly after the funeral we had an auction. We sold the farm for $1,500 and auctioned off everything that was on it. I regret that we didn't keep some items, especially mother's old spinning wheel, which held so many memories of her. After the sale I packed up my few belongings and took the train for Winnipeg. I was leaving the old farm where I had lived all my life, but I was happy that there would be no more chores.

I went to live with my sister Helen in the big city of Winnipeg. I had my own room in her nice large home. The house had hardwood floors, a parlour room for guests, a dining room with a big table and a basement for storing fruit. Best of all, it had indoor plumbing.

I had to pay Helen $25.00 a month for room and board, which meant that for the first time I had to do work outside of the farm. Thankfully, jobs were easy to find because of the war. My first job was at Christy Bakery where I worked on the assembly line labelling the bakery goods. I had to be fast but enjoyed working for a pay check. I earned about 45 cents an hour, which was better than twenty-five cents a day picking stones on the neighbor's farm.

I rode my bike to the bakery on a path that ran between two sets of train tracks. When a slow train would come along, I'd grab onto the side and let it pull me along the path to work.

Helen required that I attend the Evangelical United Brethren church with Julius and her on Sundays. Their son Walter, who was a little younger than I, also had to attend church. Neither of us liked church or believed in God. When Helen and Julius had come to visit us on the farm they would lead us in strict devotions. Walter and I would usually hide in the barn to escape. However, now that I was living with them, a rule was a rule. Even when Walter and I went to parties Saturday evening and got home after midnight, we had to get up to go to Sunday school and church. Sometimes we could hardly stay awake during the service.

One Saturday evening we went to my brother Henry's place for a party. He played the violin and we danced and drank until early in the morning. We were drinking *schmirk,* or ether. This was a very common drink back on the farm. My mother used to buy ether in a blue can with cross bones on it. It was poison but everyone drank it anyway. We mixed it with weak tea or poured some on a cup of sugar and ate it with a spoon.

After drinking all evening we were feeling pretty high. I followed Walter out to his little yellow convertible sports car and got into the

Walter Wensel and his little yellow sports car

passenger seat. Leonard was in the middle and two other girls were in the rumble seat in the back. We dropped the girls off before continuing on toward home. It was raining and combined with the effects of the ether, Walter was having trouble focusing on the road. He drove straight past a stop sign and turned left onto the main road without looking. Suddenly, a trolley bus came rushing at us, its lights glaring, the driver hammering on the horn. It slammed straight into my side of the car.

There were no seatbelts in those days and I felt myself being flung out of the car. I lay dazed on the road, blood oozing from my head as the trolley driver rushed over to us. He called an ambulance to take us to the nearby hospital. Leonard and Walter weren't seriously injured but they admitted me right away. The doctor could see that my head needed stitches. As he sewed me up all the ether I had drank at the party acted as my painkiller. The next day, the doctor came to my bed and said, "Edna, the x-rays show that you have a fractured pelvis. I'm sorry to tell you this, but you may never walk again."

My heart fell. I had always been a strong, healthy farm girl, but now what could I do? What would my life be as a cripple? I began to think about God. I had never prayed and wasn't even sure if there was a God, but now I needed help. Maybe He could heal me. I prayed, "God, if You let me walk again, I promise to follow You."

I had no idea what that promise really meant, but suddenly I had a great desire to read the Bible. I found one in the drawer of the table beside my bed and started reading in Genesis. My reading was very slow, as I had never really read a book before in my life. As I kept reading and praying, I asked God over and over to allow me to walk again.

When the specialist came to see me, I asked, "When can I go home?"

"When you finish reading the Bible," he said.

It was a joke, but I thought he was serious and I kept reading.

After six weeks I walked out of the hospital. I also walked away from God and the promise I had made. I could walk again and didn't think I needed Him. I spent the next three months in Moosehorn with Elsie recuperating. When I returned to Winnipeg, I dutifully went back to church with Helen.

During the sermon, the American speaker looked out at the congregation and said, "Someone in the audience has made a promise to God and has not kept it!"

I shifted uncomfortably in my seat. I knew he was speaking directly to me. I'd made a promise to God and hadn't kept it. When he gave the altar call at the end of the sermon, I went up to the front and the pastor's wife prayed for me. I prayed sincerely but it seemed like nothing was happening. I still felt the same. I went home and prepared for bed. I then turned off the light, threw myself on my bed and began to cry. I don't ever remember crying before, not even at my mother's funeral. Now I couldn't stop.

Suddenly, the room filled with light. "Where did it come from?" I wondered. I was amazed. Then I knew that God had come into the room and into my life. I now felt like a new person. God had indeed changed my life. Some of the changes were gradual, but the biggest change was instant. I was no longer the defiant tomboy ready to get into mischief and give the teacher a black eye. I became a bold follower of Jesus.

Yes, I was bold for Jesus and I had plenty of zeal, but I needed to learn how to share my faith. My first targets were my co-workers. I was sure they would be interested to hear what had happened to me. How wrong I was! No one wanted to hear what I had to say. Some thought that the accident had knocked some screws loose in my head. I soon made more enemies than converts. I felt discouraged and prayed for wisdom on how to share my faith.

At the time I was working in a packinghouse grading eggs in a dark room. Farmers would ship their eggs from all over Manitoba. I came up with a wonderful, creative idea to share the Gospel. I placed gospel tracts in the empty egg cases hoping the farmers would read them.

One day my foreman came to see me in the dark room where I was working. He showed me a piece of crumpled-up paper.

"Do you recognize this?" I said yes enthusiastically. It was one of the tracts that I had placed in the egg case. Proudly, I told him about my idea.

My boss looked at me for a moment then asked, "Would you like to hear what the farmer who sent me this had to say?"

"Oh yes," I said. He read what the farmer had written on the tract: "You can keep this piece of paper for your own bathroom; we already have plenty for our outhouses."

"You could get fired for this kind of thing," he said, and then walked away.

Confused, I wondered why all my attempts to share my faith had failed. I started asking questions, trying to find out where I could go to learn how to pray and share my faith. It seemed no one had any answers. Then one Sunday at church, I heard about a Bible school in Regina, Saskatchewan called Hillcrest Christian College. It sounded like a good place to learn the answers to my questions. I was very excited and the next morning I went to my boss to ask for a leave of absence to attend Bible school. He thought I said "Barber School" and gave me a three-month leave of absence to attend.

When I told Helen about Bible school, she said, "If you go, you don't have to come back and live at my house."

I couldn't understand why she was being so harsh, after she had prayed for so long for me to become a Christian. Maybe she was concerned about me leaving my job without money to pay for school.

I packed my bags, bought a train ticket and was on my way to Bible school. An ignorant farm girl with a grade four education, I had no idea what Bible school was all about. My purpose for going was to learn how to pray and share my faith. As a very new Christian I had hardly even read the Bible, let alone any other book. But I had a zeal for God even if I had very little knowledge of who He was.

Chapter 4
Fruit Begins to Show

I arrived in Regina in the middle of winter. Snow was piled as high as the railway cars and the temperature was about -40 degrees. I was told that there was no room in the school dorm so I would have to stay at the pastor's house which was about half a mile from the school. Every day in the winter I walked the distance in the deep snow and cold, windy weather.

My first class was called 'Historical Books'. Since I was starting in the second semester, I had missed 1 Chronicles. We began studying 2 Chronicles, which was about the kings of Israel and Judah. I had no idea they had kings in those days. In fact I didn't know or understand much of anything that was being taught. My mind was blank and I was sure I didn't belong in Bible school. After the class I decided to go back home.

God was faithful however. He saw my dilemma and opened a way for me. The teacher was aware of my confusion and after class she invited me to her home for the evening. She explained very simply about the kings and encouraged me to stay. I agreed to stay a little longer.

My next class was Theology. I wondered what kind of an animal a 'Theology' was; I had never heard the word before. The class was on the difference between Calvinists and Armenians. These were words I had never heard. Now I was really convinced that I was at the wrong place. I could hardly read and certainly didn't know how to spell those big words. After class, I hurried home to my room. I threw myself on the bed and cried out to God. Opening my Bible at random, I placed my finger on a verse. It fell on James 1:5: 'If anyone of you lack wisdom let him ask of God who gives to all liberally and without reproach and it will be given to him.'

I was amazed. I claimed that verse for myself and kept reminding myself of its words. Later I was told that randomly opening the Bible and pointing to a verse isn't how to find guidance, but it worked for me. From then on, I knew I was at the right place and could do anything with God's help. I studied hard and prayed often. After three months, the school moved to Medicine Hat, Alberta and I continued my studies there.

Book reviews

1. Hello Edna I am very impressed with this wonderful book.
What a tremendous job you did. I laughed and cried a lot and could not move from my chair until I read it from cover to cover.
Now I want all our friends to read it. And I loved the pictures too.

2. What a great book I could not put it down and I consumed every exiting testimony with great delight.

3. The only problem I had with the book is having to stop and wept my tears away.

4. I started reading your book beside the pool and couldn't put it down and I got severely sun burnt.

5. Hello Grandma Thanks for sending me a copy of your book.
I found it difficult to put it down, because of the constant adventure in your life. I felt as though I was taking part in your journey. Thanks for sharing your story. Love Paul

6. Wow a friend loaned me your book. It is truly inspirational. I read it as soon as she loaned it to me. And enjoyed it immensely, can't wait for the movie. Meeting Mother Theresa must have been awesome. Where can I buy a copy?

It was there that I saw and heard my first missionary. He was home on furlough from India. He told us that India was one of the hardest mission fields in the world. He explained about the caste system and how difficult it was for those caught inside it to become Christians. When I heard him say "hard" and "difficult," that old love of a challenge stirred in me. I wanted to go to India and share Jesus. I started to pray and prepare for the mission field.

After my first year at Hillcrest, I decided I wanted to go back in the fall. However, I wasn't sure where to stay over the summer though, as Helen had told me I couldn't go back to her place if I went to Bible school. I went back to my job packing egg crates in Winnipeg and stayed with my sister Emma, who was glad to have me. A few days after I arrived, Helen called to talk to me.

"Where are you?" she asked. "We've got your room all ready!"

I was embarrassed. I'd thought she didn't want me, but I couldn't very well tell her that. I said, "Well, I'm staying with Emma." I spent a week with Emma then went back to my old room at Helen's place. I returned to school in the fall.

While I was in my second year of Bible school, a request came from Reverend McNair. He ministered on several Native reservations in the Qu'Appelle Valley near Yorkton, Saskatchewan.

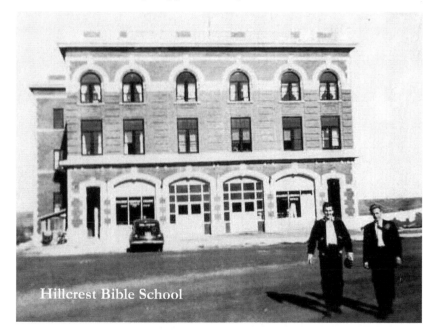

Hillcrest Bible School

He asked if some students and teachers could come and do missionary work on the reservation for the summer months. I prayed about this opportunity and thought that it would be a wonderful preparation for India. Jane Young, one of the Bible school teachers, and I volunteered to go.

After Bible school finished for the summer, we took our bikes and went by train to Yorkton. We had no idea where we would stay and we had no money for accommodations. We stopped to see the government representatives who lived near the reserve. They were a very nice couple and welcomed us with open arms.

They suggested that we stay in a small cabin near their house on the reserve. We didn't hesitate to accept their invitation and moved in. There was a wood stove for cooking and the couple who had made the offer provided us with a bed and a desk. All we had to do was acquire a few pots and pans. This cabin would be our home for the next four months.

Me in the Qu'Appelle Valley

Anxious to meet the natives who lived on the reserve, we rode our bikes to visit their homes. They welcomed us to the reserve and in turn we invited them to visit our cabin. Soon quite a few people were stopping by, especially the young men our age. We decided to stay focused on ministry and not men, but they were helpful with the odd jobs that needed to be done.

We arranged services for Sunday at 11:00 a.m. We soon discovered that the native people arrived on their own time, along with their dogs and kids. We soon got used to the distractions. We also arranged children's clubs in different homes. There were also unexpected events like funerals. We would attend the wake then have a service after the Catholic priest had held mass.

Jane and I worked together quite well and had a very exciting and adventurous summer. One day while Jane and I were walking through the bushes, we came across a strange plant.

Jane said, "It's poison ivy, Edna. Stay away from it!"

Poison Ivy Reaction

"Oh, I'm not afraid of poison ivy," I said. To prove my point I broke off some of the plant and rubbed it on my fingers. Nothing happened. I then put my hands on my face as Jane watched me in horror. The next morning, my face had swollen so badly I couldn't see out of my eyes. It took a week for the swelling to go down. I never touched poison ivy again.

God was faithful and supplied all of our needs, even more than we could ask or think. While we saw very few tangible results from our ministry, we sowed lots of seeds and we knew that we had made a difference in some of their lives, especially with the children.

We left one month before it was time to go back to Bible school. Jane went home to visit her family while I decided to visit my nephew Henry in La Fleche, Saskatchewan. He had a large farm and harvest was in full swing. Shortly after I arrived, his hired man quit because of a drinking problem. New help was hard to find during harvest, so Henry asked me,

"Can you drive a truck?"

"Of course," I said. I had only driven a car once or twice but, to me, it was just another challenge.

"Do you want to help me get in the harvest?"

"Yes," I said, delighted at the opportunity.

My first day on the job, Henry asked me to drive the truck up a steep incline close to a creek. I had no idea how to use the clutch, brakes and gas all at the same time. The truck started rolling back toward the creek. I tried several times to get it to go up the incline without success. I pulled and pushed on the various pedals and levers, but the truck kept sliding backwards. Henry was watching from close by. As the truck kept rolling back he came up and asked calmly,

"Do you need any help?"

Tears were starting in my eyes. "Yes, I need help."

With a good-humored smile on his face, he got into the driver's seat. Without any difficulty, he drove the truck to level ground.

"Now it's your turn," he said, getting out.

He had more confidence in my driving than I had, but I got back in the truck and learned to drive the truck both uphill and down.

Before Henry arrived at 5:00 a.m. to start each day, I had to get up at 4:00 a.m. and grease the combine. I had to grease it again at lunchtime and haul the grain in the truck from the combine to the elevator, which was about four miles away. My workday ended at about 8:00 at night. I was a fast learner and had no more close calls or accidents.

I worked hard for the month, enjoying the challenge. I wasn't sure how much Henry would pay me, but I knew that he was generous and fair. He told me again and again that he was pleased with my work. The last day of harvest, he drove me to Regina to catch the train for Medicine Hat. Smiling at me, he said,

"Thanks for all the help you've given me this summer." He handed me an envelope. When I got on the train, I opened it. There was a check with enough money to cover my school year and even some for spending. I was stunned. God is good.

My third year of Bible school was the hardest yet, but I studied hard and prayed often. After the school year ended, I wanted to go back to the reserve but Jane was unable to go with me. I needed help if I was to be there again. Two of my best friends, Lenora and Louise, volunteered to go. They were both talented in music, which was a blessing, because I couldn't carry a tune in a clothesbasket.

When I arrived at Bible school I'd joined the choir. After the second practice, I was kindly asked to drop out. I wondered why, because I didn't know I couldn't sing. I decided to take piano lessons instead. After a month, I was asked to play for chapel. I practiced one simple hymn really well, but when I got in front of all the students and staff I got nervous and missed some notes, then lost my place on the music sheet. I was so embarrassed I never took another lesson. Next I took voice lessons, but that didn't help either, so I gave up on my music career. We decided that Lenora and Louise would take care of the music and I'd do the preaching.

Louise, Lenora and I

Before we left school, God provided us with an old Ford coupe car. We were excited to have a car and not have to go up and down those steep hills on bikes. We drove the car to the reserve without trouble and were welcomed back with open arms. We were able to stay in the same small house on the reserve and continue the same type of ministry. Having a car made it easier to visit the people more often. Some of the seeds that we had sown the year before bore fruit and we soon had a small group of believers.

One of the believers, Eddie Stonechild, was quite a mature Christian and could preach like a house on fire. Our principal told us that the school would like to sponsor a native student if we could find one who was willing to attend Bible school. Well, Eddie was eager to leave the reserve and attend Bible school. After a good summer, we left the reserve and drove back to the Bible school with Eddie. Eddie was quite a hit with the principal and staff. He was a good speaker and was asked to speak in several churches. Then one day he skipped classes, went to town, got drunk, came back to the school and beat up his roommate. The principal called the police and they came and took him away. It was a sad ending for someone we'd been so proud of.

When I arrived at school for my fourth and last year I had no money to pay my fees. I wondered how God would supply the money and I prayed a lot and worried a little. After two weeks, I went to the office to explain that I still didn't have the money to pay for my fee but that I would continue to pray until God provided me with money.

I thought I might be asked to leave the school, but instead the secretary smiled and said, "I have something for you, Edna." She handed me a piece of paper. It was a receipt saying, "Paid in full." An anonymous person had paid all my school fees. After three and-a-half difficult years, I graduated with honours.

Top, third from the left is me, 6th from the left is Alfred and 9th from the left is Roy Hehr my soon to be brother-in law.

Chapter 5
A Changing Dream

After my first year at Bible school, two of my friends from my church in Winnipeg and I went to a church camp meeting in Saskatchewan. We took a tent along because there wasn't enough room for us to stay in the cabins.

"Where should we pitch the tent?" my friend Lillian asked.

"Here, by the trail," I said. As we tried to set up the tent, it kept collapsing.

"Do you need help?" Looking up, I saw a tall, handsome young man watching us struggle with the tent.

"Yes, thank you," I said

"You know, you shouldn't put the tent so close to the trail," he said.

"It'll be fine," I said. In the morning, we discovered people streaming around our tent on their way to the meeting. Sure enough, the three of us had to call the young man, whose name was Alfred Adam, to help us take the tent down and pitch it somewhere else. After it was set up again, we were invited to go swimming with some friends. I invited Alfred to go along. We all had a good time swimming. Later that evening Alfred and I went for a walk.

"I'm going to Bible school in Medicine Hat," I told him. "I want to become a missionary in India.

"That's wonderful," he said.

After our walk, he came into the tent and we talked for hours completely forgetting about the ten o'clock curfew. Then we heard a voice outside our tent. "Alfred?"

Alfred's pastor had come by to check if everybody was in his or her tents. Sheepishly, Alfred emerged from our tent. The pastor grinned and winked at me.

"It's past ten o' clock, Alfred."

Alfred was a new Christian and very sincere about keeping all the rules at camp. He apologized to his pastor and promised to keep all the rules. In the next few days, we took more walks and shared our thoughts and future plans. Then our pastor, Reverend Gaurke, got a call: someone in our congregation had died and he had to perform the funeral. He was the one who had brought us to the camp, so we had to leave early with him. Before I left, Alfred asked me for my address. Shortly after I arrived home, I found a card from him. He wrote and told me that he had decided to attend Hillcrest too. I wasn't sure what his motive was, but we agreed to meet in Regina and travel together by train to school.

At school, Alfred and I became good friends. We were both interested in missions but I wanted to go to India and he wanted to go to Africa. I wasn't looking for a serious relationship because I wanted to go to India as a single missionary. Nevertheless, we kept seeing more and more of each other.

The school was strict about students dating and Alfred had to ask the principal for permission to take me out on a date. We were allowed to go out once a month with the condition that we go to a respectable place like the Salvation Army. Alfred was very conscientious about the rules and wouldn't even walk me up the girls' steps of the dorm.

One night at the Salvation Army, we watched a movie called "The King of Kings." At the end of the movie, the words appeared on the screen: "Go ye into all the world and preach the Gospel." I looked over at Alfred and saw that he was crying.

As we walked back to the dorms, I said, "Why were you crying tonight, Alfred?"

He paused for a moment and then he said, "When those words came on the screen, everything went pitch black, just like a black velvet sheet had been pulled across the screen. Then a map of India appeared, with a map of Africa in the background. Edna, this is my call to go to India."

As we continued walking home, I knew I wasn't as happy as he expected me to be. I had planned to go to India as a single person, but now I would have to make a choice.

The next day I talked to Alfred and said, "I need some time to pray about our relationship."

He was devastated. He was sure that we were meant for each other so he began to fast and pray. I asked everyone, both teachers and friends, whether they thought he was right for me. I didn't know how I was supposed to feel about him. Everyone encouraged me towards marrying him.

"If you don't want him, I'll have him," Jane said.

But I was still unsure. I didn't understand Alfred's agony and in my insensitivity, let space grow between us. One evening I saw him come through the door all dressed up in his graduation suit.

"What a handsome fellow," I thought.

Until then, I'd never really seen it. I was falling in love with him. Not only that, but my desire to go to India on my own had changed. I knew at last that Alfred and I were meant for each other. However, by this time he was ignoring me and had asked another girl out. How could I tell him?

I came up with an idea. I had stored my bike at the apartment he shared with his brother Herald and his sister Mary. As they were both in class, I knew Alfred would be home alone, so I walked over to his apartment and knocked on the door.

Alfred opened the door and stared at me. Feeling terribly awkward and nervous, I said, "I've come to check on my bike."

He pointed to the corner and said coldly, "It's over there."

Pretending to look my bike over, I avoided Alfred's stare and made my way back to the door. This was awful. Then, with a surge of bravery, I turned towards him and looked him in the eyes.

"Alfred, I want to make up with you. I'm sorry for breaking up; I really think we're meant for each other."

His eyes widened. "If you really mean it, let's set a date for the wedding." We set the date for August 19th, 1950. There were a few weeks before graduation, so we spent lots of quality time together. After graduating in April, we got married in August as planned.

Reverend Guarke married us in my home church in Winnipeg. My sister Helen and the ladies of the church took care of all the preparations, making food and hanging streamers across the reception hall. I couldn't afford to buy a new wedding dress so I borrowed one from my friend. Alfred wore a blue suit. All the bridesmaids dressed in long, colourful dresses and we carried bouquets of roses and ribbons. Elsie, Helen, Emma and Leonard came to the wedding, along with many of my friends.

After the wedding we went to Saskatchewan for a short honeymoon. It was harvest time so during the honeymoon Alfred had to work in the field and most of the time I rode on the tractor with him. After the honeymoon Alfred stayed to finish the harvest. I went back to Winnipeg to pack up my things and left by bus for Toronto where I had enrolled in a one year, condensed nurse's training course.

I rented a one-bedroom suite in Toronto and started the program. One month later Alfred arrived. We bought an old van for him to go to work as a bricklayer and a motorized bike for me to go to school. Nurse's training was very hard and many times I was tempted to quit, but I knew it was important to have the training before going to India. I rode that motorized bike to the hospital every day, rain or snow. Many times it would stall and I would have to push it in the rush hour traffic, but I never gave up.

That first Christmas Alfred's parents sent us half a pig wrapped in a gunnysack. We had no idea what to do with half a pig. We didn't have a fridge or freezer so we buried it in a snow bank until we could use it. Because Elsie had done all the housework when I was young, I didn't even know how to boil water without burning it. I don't remember what we did with the pig after the snow melted. With time, I learned to cook and make the most of a tight budget. Soon I became pregnant and we needed a bigger place. We rented a two- bedroom basement suite close to the nursing school.

I had a difficult pregnancy and had to drop out of nurse's training before the course ended. Six weeks overdue, on July 26, 1951, I finally went into labour in the middle of the night. Alfred helped me into our old van and started the engine. It was so late we were the only vehicle on the road. The engine began to cough.

"What's wrong, Al?" I asked.

"I don't know." The engine sputtered one last time, then died. Alfred pulled over to the side of the road. My contractions were coming closer together.

"You okay, Edna?"

"What are we going to do?"

"Hope a car comes soon."

We watched out the window at the road stretching out on either end of us, but it remained dark. The pain was becoming intense, my breathing heavy.

"What if the baby comes first?"

"We need to pray," Alfred said, taking my hands.

"Lord, send us a car – soon."

Just then, two lights appeared on the road, coming towards

Alfred flung open the door and waved at the car. "Stop! Stop! Over here!"

The car slowed and pulled up beside us. A young man got out." What's wrong?"

"My wife's having a baby and our van broke down on the way to the hospital."

"You don't say. I'm coming from the hospital where my wife just had a baby. Let's get your wife in the car."

Safely at the hospital, I endured hard labour for 32 hours until I was completely exhausted. Finally, the doctor delivered the baby with forceps. On July 28, 1951 we had a lovely daughter, weighing over nine pounds. We named her Fern Louise after one of the nurses at the school and she was the pride and joy of our lives.

Alfred, Fern and I
1951

Chapter 6
Living by Faith

Shortly after Fern was born we joined Worldwide Evangelical Crusade (WEC) to begin our missionary training. After Alfred and I had broken up while at Hillcrest, we had both applied separately to WEC, without knowing the other intended to do so. We had both been accepted as singles, but after we got married, they told us we would have to wait for a year to adjust to marriage before we could take our training. After a year in Toronto we moved to Beamsville, Ontario, where the Canadian headquarters for WEC was located. We had very little money and trusted God for all of our needs. One day I had to make a phone call, but didn't even have one nickel for the call. "God, send me a nickel," I prayed. Just then, in walked an officer from the Salvation Army. He came up to Fern, who smiled at him.

"Here you go." He handed her a shiny nickel.

"Thank You God!" I prayed silently, and then I made the call. I was convinced that faith really does work. We knew then that God would supply all our needs.

After a year in Beamsville we were asked to move to the Mission Headquarters in Chicago. We arrived in July and it was very hot, especially in the mission kitchen where I worked. The training at mission headquarters was very difficult, especially for me with a young child. Shortly after we arrived Fern became very ill with a rash and a high fever of 107. As we watched her become more and more sick we prayed earnestly for the fever to subside.

"You need to take her to the doctor," the WEC staff said. Alfred and I looked at each other. We knew we didn't have any money to pay for a doctor. Yet Fern's temperature remained high.

"Alfred, we need to take her in," I said. "Let's trust God to provide the money."

The doctor diagnosed Fern with roseola and prescribed antibiotics, which brought down her fever. God supplied the money for the doctor and the medication.

While Fern recovered, I had to continue working in the kitchen. Most of the staff at headquarters were old maids, but that didn't stop them from giving me advice about how to take care of Fern. One Sunday morning, I took Fern to the kitchen where she slept in the baby carriage. A staff member walked through the kitchen on the way to church and said, "This child should not be in the kitchen. Take her to your room."

"Alright," I said and pushed her back to our room.

No sooner had I got her settled again when there was a knock on my door.

"Edna! Why aren't you in the kitchen? You're supposed to be working."

I put Fern in the carriage again and took her back to the kitchen. As I started working, yet another staff member walked through the kitchen.

"Why is your baby here in the kitchen? She's been so ill, she needs to be out in the sun." So I pushed Fern's carriage outside into the sunshine, where I could keep an eye on her. Then everyone began coming back from church. One by one, the women came into the kitchen and confronted me.

"How could you leave your baby out in the hot sun? Take her back in the kitchen!"

I took a deep breath and went outside to bring Fern in. I knew I was about to lose my temper and explode. What did they know about raising babies? I had had enough.

"Edna." I spun around, ready to get angry. It was Alfred, returned from church.

"How was your morning?" he asked.

Tears jumped into my eyes, then I started crying. "Horrible. I've had enough!"

"Well, let's go get some food. It's time for lunch."

We lined up for our food. In front of us was the mission leader, who turned around and said something sarcastic. That did it; I burst into tears again.

"I can't do anything right! I've had it!"

To the leader, this outburst meant I was certainly not missionary material. We were sent back to the Canadian headquarters with the recommendation that we weren't fit to be missionaries. Fortunately, the staff in Canada was very sympathetic when they heard our side of the story and welcomed us back to Beamsville. We worked hard and cooperated with the staff, remaining there until our second child was born.

This time labour was a very different experience. When I went into labour Hebrews 12:2 came to mind: "… looking unto Jesus, the author and finisher of our faith, who for the joy that was set before Him endured the cross."

"I'll endure this pain for the joy of having a baby," I thought. While I was rejoicing in this revelation the nurse leaned over me.

"Do you want something for the pain?" I looked up at her, confused.

"What pain?"

The pain had disappeared, replaced by joy over having another baby. Daniel Alfred was born on Dec. 20, 1952. He weighed ten pounds! We took him home on Christmas Day and everyone at the headquarters rejoiced with us.

One day one of the staff smelled a terrible odour coming from the basement. Going down the stairs, he found that a family of skunks had moved in. The staff called a meeting to discuss how to get rid of the skunks without making the situation worse.

"I have an idea," Alfred said.

He constructed a box that had a window in the back and a trap door in the front. Then he hung some food near the window. The skunk would enter the box to try to reach the food, then the trap door would close behind it and the skunk would be caught with its tail pinned between its legs, unable to spray scent. The trap worked so well he eventually caught the whole family of seven skunks. After they were in the trap, he took the box with the skunks and placed it behind the car with the exhaust fumes going into the box, killing the skunks without any odour or pain. This made him a hero with the staff.

We continued to work doing outreach and evangelism and, when our training finished, we were sent to the mission headquarters in Philadelphia for final approval. After spending a short time in Philadelphia we were accepted as missionaries for India. Although we had no money for our ship fare or for our time in India, WEC was a faith mission and didn't require that we have support beforehand. Their policy was that, if God had truly called

us, then He would provide for our needs. We were both very excited and could hardly wait to get to India.

We managed to get a booking on a freighter leaving from New York to Bombay (Mumbai) in a few months. While waiting, we planned a trip to the west coast to visit churches and say goodbye to family and friends. Then I found out I was pregnant with our third child. The mission policy at the time was that new missionaries shouldn't have more than two children before going to the mission field because that would make it too hard to study a new language and adjust to a new country. We still wanted to go so we decided not to tell the mission about the pregnancy.

We had very little money to get to the west coast, so we purchased an old car at an auto wrecker's shop for sixty dollars. We didn't have enough money to pay for repairs if the car broke down, but we believed that God would get us there safely.

Just before leaving for the west coast, Alfred said to me, "God told me He's going to give us a brown Ford car."

We were very excited, wondering just when and how we would get the car. Before leaving, we were scheduled to speak at a nearby church and thought that perhaps someone at the church would give us the car. Alfred said I should get my driver's license so I could drive one of the cars back from church. After we shared our message, the church gave us a small offering, but no car. Although we were disappointed, we knew God had a car somewhere for us. We just needed to trust Him and wait for his timing.

We started our journey in our old junkyard car, driving to our next stop. Reverend Guarke was now pastoring a church near Chicago and had invited us to stay at his place so we could share at his church. We spoke at the meeting and once again received a small offering. The next morning we loaded all our things in the old car, ready to drive to Winnipeg.

Just before we pulled away from the Reverend Guarke's house his wife looked at our car and asked, "Are you sure this old car will get you to the west coast?"

"Of course we're sure. God will look after us," Alfred said with confidence.

She turned to her husband and whispered in his ear. He nodded his head. She said, "We bought a car for our daughter to use while she went to university, but she didn't need it so it's just sitting in our garage. We'd like to give it to you."

"What make is it?" Alfred asked.

"It's a 1949 Ford."

"What color?"

"Brown."

He looked at me and smiled, then turned to the couple. "This is the car God promised me."

We immediately went to get the title transferred, then left with both cars for Winnipeg, Alfred in the new (to us) Ford and me driving the old car. As we kept driving into the night, it grew later and later. Unused to driving at night, I felt myself drifting off at the wheel. I signalled to Alfred to pull over. "I have to take a nap, or I'll fall asleep."

We pulled over on the side of the road and stretched out on the seats to sleep. We hadn't been asleep for long when a car pulled up beside us.

"Excuse me sir, ma'am."

We sat up. It was the highway patrol. "We need to ask you some questions. What are you doing parked here?"

"It was getting too late to keep driving and we had to sleep."

"Why do you have two cars – one Canadian, one American?"

"Well, we're married and ……"

"Do both these cars belong to you?"

"Yes, you see, we just had the Ford given to us."

We explained the story and they let us continue. The next morning, we arrived at the Canadian border.

"Sorry, but there's no way you can take an American car across the border."

"Sir," Alfred said, "This car was a gift. We need it to get back to the west coast."

"I'm sorry sir, but that's the law and there's nothing I can do."

We had no choice but to leave our new car at a church near the border. As we traveled to Winnipeg in our old car, we wondered how we could get the Ford back. Surely God wouldn't have provided it only to take it away again. In Winnipeg we decided to try again at the office for Customs and Immigration.

"Sorry, but you'll never get your car across," they said. "Only one person ever got an American car across the border and he was a Mormon missionary."

Together, we prayed, "God, we want to be the second missionaries to get a car across the border. You gave us this car, so we know You can help us get it across."

We continued to speak to the people in the office, trying to win their favour. Finally they said, "Alright, you can take your car across the border. But if you ever decide to sell it, you have to take it back to the States."

Triumphant, we went back to get our Ford and drove it across the border. We had a great trip and spoke in many churches. At the end of our trip we had enough money for our ship fare, but we still had no support promised for our time in India. On our way to the ship we stopped back at the Canadian headquarters in Beamsville. The pastor asked us to share at the Sunday morning service before leaving. On Saturday night he couldn't sleep because he couldn't stop wondering whether we had enough support for India. Early Sunday morning he called our mission leader and asked him how much support we had for India. The leader told him we had none.

The pastor called his elders together for an urgent meeting. He told them about our need and said, "We need to help."

They all agreed and promised to give us $250 a year for as long as we were in India. The pastor gave us the news at the Sunday morning service. We were overwhelmed and wondered what we would do with all that money. Throughout our time in India, the church not only sent us the money, but also prayed and sent us parcels with food and other items.

Our next stop was at our headquarters in Philadelphia, where we gathered things from the missionary barrel to take to India. We found lots of toys and clothes for our children but nothing for Alfred and me. Then we received a message. A wealthy Christian friend of WEC had called to ask if anyone was leaving for the mission field. They told her we were leaving soon for India. She sent her chauffeur to pick us up for dinner. She had a beautiful, large home with servants and we had a wonderful meal and good Christian fellowship. In the dining room there was even a button on the floor she could press to call the servants. At the end of the evening, she asked us, "Are you free to go shopping tomorrow?"

The next day, her chauffeur picked us up again and took us to her home. Before we went shopping she asked,

"Edna, we must be about the same size. Do you want to look at my clothes and see if there's anything you can use?"

Her clothes were all brand name and expensive. I chose several suits, which fit me beautifully. Then we went to the shopping mall to shop for my husband. She outfitted him with new shoes that cost $35, $30 more than we would have spent and many shirts, pants and socks.

Meeting this wealthy lady, we thought that we had found the goose that laid the golden egg and that she would look after us while in India. Assuming we would never lack anything again, we took our eyes off God and looked to her for our needs. To our disappointment, we never heard from her again. Hers was a one-time generosity, which she performed for many missionaries. We had to humble ourselves, repent, and get our eyes back on God.

Chapter 7
To the East

It was finally time to sail for India. We left God's car at the mission headquarters for other missionaries to use while home on furlough and had someone drive us to New York. The cheapest fare we could get was on an old freighter, which took six weeks to get to Bombay. The first day aboard it was calm and peaceful. Then that night, the wind picked up and the sea began to shift the boat back and forth. I became seasick and, compounded with morning sickness, I often 'fed the fish' as Alfred said, a dozen times a day.

There were only twelve passengers on the ship. Being a freighter, it stopped at many ports - Iraq, Iran and Lebanon. These ports were all trouble spots so we weren't allowed to go ashore. In Iraq however, Alfred managed to go ashore. He was hoping to find the Garden of Eden, so he hired a cab. The driver took him on a wild

Daniel, Me and Fern

goose chase and they never found the Garden of Eden.

I continued to have morning sickness and seasickness. Some days I wanted to die. "Is this what a missionary's life is like?" I wondered.

I became depressed and couldn't sleep at night. Alfred was concerned and prayed that God would heal me. I did get some relief and was able to sleep better, but I was still a long way from being well.

Finally we arrived in Bombay. It felt so good to put my feet on solid ground after six weeks on the rough seas. We spent a couple of days in Bombay at the Salvation Army. We still were a long ways from our destination of Darjeeling, near the Nepal border, and we had no idea how long it would take us to get there by train. After looking at a map, we chose the shortest and cheapest route, not knowing that the shortest route wasn't the best choice. We would have to change trains many times.

Traveling by train in India was a nightmare. We traveled third class - because there was no fourth class - with no reservations. We had all our belongings with us, consisting of two 40-gallon barrels and several suitcases. We wanted to make sure we had enough to last six years, so we'd brought clothes, bedding, cookware and many other items.

We were traveling during the season of a holy pilgrimage, when the Hindus travelled in droves to the Ganges River along the same route we had chosen. At every station, there were thousands of people waiting for the train to arrive. In India, the first ones on get the seats, so people run to meet the train and get on before it even stops. With so much luggage and two small children, we had to wait for the train to stop then push our way on.

The trains were terribly crowded with people sitting wherever they could find room. Not only that, there were bedbugs everywhere. People showed us how to put newspapers around us to keep away the bedbugs at night, because they were deterred by light colors. We were told not to eat on the train so we packed a lunch before we left Bombay. That was all the food we had until we got to Kurseong.

After four days on the train, I at last saw the Himalayan foothills. Jake Dyck, our senior missionary, was waiting in Siliguri to take us up the hills to Kurseong. Our nightmare on the train was over. Seeing a familiar white face, I began to weep.

Kurseong is 4864 ft. above sea level, near Darjeeling. While there we stayed upstairs in Jake and Helen's house. It had a tin roof and a winding road leading up to it through the terraced tea plantations surrounding our house. During the day, we would watch the women in their colourful saris go through the bright green rows picking tea leaves off the bushes and putting them into baskets held on around their heads by a cloth strap. Sometimes a woman would go into labour and have her baby in the field, then continue working.

A few days after we arrived in Kurseong, we began studying the Nepali language. We hired a local teacher who spoke only a little English and soon we were able to speak some Nepalese, practicing on our ayah, Bina, who helped with the children.

When I was near my due date for our third child, we had to leave Kurseong and drive the 30 miles up to Darjeeling, where there was a hospital. We rented a place while we waited for the baby to arrive. After a few weeks of waiting, I finally went into labour. In India, they gave nothing for pain during labour. As I lay there in agony, the missionary woman who had come with me said, "Oh, quit your complaining, people have babies all the time."

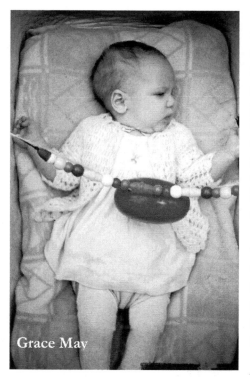
Grace May

Thankfully, the birth was faster than my first two and on May 27th, 1954 baby Grace May was delivered safely. She was a beautiful precious baby and her name Grace was meant for her. God was to give her a heart full of abounding Grace. She was to be a source of blessing to all those who enter into her home.

Our Missions' leader was visiting from the States and came to the hospital to visit my new baby and me. Soon after Grace was born we returned to Kurseong to continue language study.

One evening while we were having prayer with the Dykes downstairs, we heard strange noises coming from upstairs. It sounded like someone was flushing the toilet. Our children were too young to flush the toilet, so we went upstairs to see what was happening. All the children were in bed and we couldn't figure out what had caused the sounds.

Back downstairs; we heard the same noises again. When we rushed upstairs, it stopped; when we went downstairs, we heard it again. It sounded very spooky. We went downstairs and prayed for God to show us where the noises were coming from.

The next morning we searched the house, even looking at the space under the tin roof to see if an animal could have got in, but found no answers. We decided that the house must be haunted, so we prayed and took authority over the spirits that were causing the disturbances. We never heard noises again.

Later, the locals said, "Do you know your house is haunted? No one would live in it; that's why the rent is so cheap. How is it that you've stayed there so long?"

"We prayed and took authority over the spirits," we told them, "and they left."

One day, a sadhu came to visit with the Dycks, barefoot and wearing the saffron robes of a Hindu ascetic. He said he felt he should search for peace, so he vowed not to stop walking barefoot until he found it. After visiting many Hindu temples in India, he then visited the Buddhist temples, walking barefoot all the way, but he still couldn't find peace. Then he walked barefoot to Mecca, hoping to find peace in the Muslim mosques, but he couldn't find peace there either. He had spent two years walking barefoot and had just entered India, preparing to go around a second time visiting the Hindu temples again. He was sure that this time he would find peace.

Jake told him, "Stop searching – you won't find peace that way. You need to accept Jesus, the Prince of Peace."

The sadhu looked at Jake and said, "That's too simple." He continued on his barefoot search for peace and we never saw him again. We heard another story of a man who had vowed not to open his hand until he found peace. He held his hand closed for so long that the nails grew through his palm and out the back of his hand. Eventually he became a Christian and found peace, but his hand was deformed.

After one year of language study, we became restless and wanted to move out on our own.

The Dykes didn't think we were ready, but secretly we planned to leave as soon as possible.

One day an Indian man came to our house and told our ayah, Bina, who was outside in the yard, "At this time next year you will be dead."

Then he came and knocked on our door. Alfred opened the door; we could tell by the man's orange turban that he was a soothsayer.

"Let me tell you your fortune," he said.

"We don't believe in your predictions," Alfred said. Alfred tried to close the door on him, but he stuck his foot in the door and said, "You have secretly planned to leave Kurseong. Now let me tell your future."

We were tempted to hear more but knew that he had the wrong spirit. As he'd said, Bina had an accident the next year and died. If he'd told us the things that would happen to us when we left Kurseong, we probably never would have gone.

Shortly after this encounter, our mission received a request to send missionaries to Pedong, the last checkpoint in India before Tibet. Since no one else was available we were asked to go. Excited to be going out on our own, we made our preparations and set off.

Pedong was a small village situated on the historical Silk Road, which goes from India to Tibet through the Himalayas, along the Jelepla Pass. During our stay it was a stopover for Tibetans bringing their wool into India. They parked their mules right next door to our house. We watched the processions of mules come down the trail, as many as a hundred at a time. The lead mule was decorated with ribbons and bells to scare away evil spirits. The Tibetans were very friendly, even allowing our children to ride on the mules. At feeding

Fern and Tibetan **Woman**

time, the sound of the mules eating their grain was like rushing water.

We lived upstairs in a Bhutanese house with a tin roof. When it rained during monsoon, the noise was very loud on the roof. The house was elevated on poles, leaving a space beneath the house for people to keep their animals, although we had no animals for ours.

We began having Gospel meetings in the market place. The people were very friendly and we soon planted a small church.

One day a Hindu couple brought a very sick young girl to our door. They had taken her to the Hindu temple, the Buddhist priests and the witch doctor. No one could help her. Hearing about the Christian God, they had brought her to us for help.

"If your God heals our daughter, we will worship Him," they said.

We prayed for the girl but saw no results, so they went home. When they got home, they sent us word that their daughter was asking for food but all they could afford was rice swept off the floor of the rice shop. We sent them over some chicken noodle soup. When we went to pray for the girl again, Alfred had a vision of a black rubber ball rolling down the hill. He saw the family searching everywhere for the ball, but they couldn't find it. He knew that it must have been a gift if it was so important.

"Have you ever had a black ball?" Alfred asked them.

"Yes," they said. "It was a gift, but it rolled away down a hill and we couldn't find it."

"Just as that ball rolled away, never to be found, so your daughter's sickness will be rolled away," Alfred said.

The girl was healed and she and her family became Christians. They are now elders in the church and one of their sons is the pastor of the church that we planted. We saw many miracles of healing in that village and that one church has multiplied to many churches.

Miracles of healing happened in our own family too. Grace shoved something sharp into her ear and punctured her eardrum. The local doctor told us to take her to Calcutta immediately for surgery. Calcutta was a long way and we didn't have the money, so we prayed for a miracle and God healed Grace.

Since Pedong was a very small village, we had a hard time finding a good ayah (nanny) to help with our three small children.

At first we hired a young local girl to help. One day we arrived home early from ministering on the streets. We found baby Grace sitting on top of the stairs with a big butcher's knife in her tiny hand. We were horrified and dismissed our ayah immediately. Afraid something similar would happen again, we didn't want to replace her with another local girl.

We wrote to our senior missionaries in Kurseong and shared our dilemma with them. They read our letter to Rajani, a lovely young lady from Nepal. We had met her while living in Kurseong and she had become a good friend. After hearing about our request, she told the missionaries that she had a dream the night before about us and a church steeple. She felt that this request was a confirmation that she should come and help us with the kids. They were amazed that Rajani, a high caste Hindu who'd told us she was married to a government worker, would want to be our ayah. (In fact, she was unmarried but had run away to escape having to marry her brother-in-law.) They wrote us to ask if we wanted her to be our ayah. We were thrilled and asked them to send her as soon as possible.

Rajani was a wonderful, reliable ayah. After working for us for about a year, she became a Christian and was baptized. One day she asked us for permission to go and visit her uncle and his family in Darjeeling. She wanted to share with him about her faith in Jesus. We gave her permission and she left for Darjeeling. When she told them that she'd become a Christian, they threatened to kill her. She

Rajani's Wedding

told us she'd heard them sharpening the knives in the kitchen to kill her and she barely escaped with her life. Despite these threats, she loved Jesus and continued to study the Bible.

After about two years, we sent her to Bible school on the plains. While she was there, she met a wonderful Bhutanese Christian man. After graduating, they got married and pastored a church in Ghum, near Darjeeling. God blessed them with three children.

While we were in Pedong, we were under such spiritual attack that Alfred felt we needed to see the word of God confirmed with signs and wonders. We didn't see any miracles happening at the time. Every morning he would get up at three a.m. and pray until breakfast, but he didn't hear anything from God. After three months, God finally spoke to him, saying, "I have heard your prayer and I am pleased with your commitment. I am giving you a fresh anointing to go and preach the Gospel and I will confirm My Word with signs and wonders."

Shortly after this experience, we heard about an evangelist conducting healing meetings in our area. Alfred attended several meetings. One evening a call was given for backsliders to come back to God. Our cook's husband, who had two children with venereal disease and had left his family, ran to the altar to ask God for forgiveness. We had been praying for this man so Alfred was very excited. As he watched this man repent, Alfred had a deep experience of God's anointing and presence. He invited the evangelist to come to Pedong for some meetings. As word spread, all kinds of people came to the meeting from surrounding villages. The sick they brought were healed and revival broke out.

Our Methodist friends, Ernie and Edie Shingler, were in Pedong studying the Tibetan language and culture. They were very impressed by what they saw at these meetings. Ernie prostrated himself on the floor to pray. Normally a very calm man, he suddenly began praying in German.

Alfred, who understood German, said, "Ernie, stop! Do you know what you're saying?"

"No, I don't."

"You're speaking in German. You're saying, Jesus' name is the stick that beats Satan over the head and the blood of Jesus is the power that defeats Satan and the power of darkness." Ernie was British and had never spoken in German before. We all repeated what he had said and felt the presence of God.

I was pregnant with my fourth child at the time and with all the spiritual intensity, I found that after awhile I needed to get away for rest. Alfred made arrangements for me to stay with a Swedish couple in Kalimpong, a nearby hill station. One night as I lay in bed I had a vision of an angel coming to me with a glass.

I asked, "Is that the good spirit, or the bad spirit?"

"It's the good spirit," the angel replied.

"Then I want a glass full."

The angel took me into the room beside mine and showed me a map on the table. It told me, "This is where your future ministry will be – in the Land of Roses." I didn't know it at the time, but it was a map of California. Feeling at peace, I returned home. Shortly before

I went into labour, Ernie gave a prophecy about me: "All will be well and you will have a son."

I had to go early to Kalimpong where there was a hospital and stay with our mission leaders the Booths until it was time for me to deliver. When I went to the hospital, Edie and Ernie were on their

Timothy and I

way to the plains below to hold revival meetings. They were still unsure if everything that was happening was from God, so they waited before getting on the bus to see if Ernie's prophecy about my baby would be true. When I delivered a boy, Timothy John, on April 13, 1956, they were delighted and took their bus to continue on. Their meetings were full of more of God's signs and wonders. I was delighted to have another son.

Shortly after Tim was born I returned to Pedong and we continued with our ministry. We planted a church in Pedong, which in the last fifty years has multiplied to many more. Our fruit remained and has borne more fruit.

Six months later, I became pregnant again. When it was time to give birth again, I had to go to Kalimpong and wait. Ruth Esther was born on December 31, 1957 without any complications. Ruth was a beautiful baby girl.

After a few years, we moved to Kalimpong. As a Buddhist religious centre, Kalimpong was filled with colourful prayer flags

Ruth Esther

fluttering on hilltops and from buildings and we became familiar with the sound of Buddhists chanting, "Oh Mani Padni Ho" ("Oh the jewel of the lotus"), banging prayer drums and turning their prayer wheels 107 times for each sin.

When China invaded Tibet, the Dalai Lama and his cabinet had to flee and they came to Kalimpong. The Panchen Lama, who was the Dalai Lama's right-hand man, acted as his medium and would go into a trance to receive messages for him. The repeated trances had taken a toll on his body and had left him in the hospital in Kalimpong, bent up and crippled. Our friends Ernie and Edie went to pray with him and gave him a Bible. We stayed in Kalimpong for about a year and studied second-year Nepali.

After we sent Rajani to Bible school, we needed another ayah. We found a girl named Maya Lata who lived with her sister and father in a small village near Kalimpong. She was a wonderful ayah and a fast learner. She soon became fluent in English and almost every day she and I had Bible study together. Soaking it up, she became a Christian and wanted to be baptized. After her baptism, she changed her name to Mary Lata. Our kids loved her and she was like a second mother to them. When we moved from Kalimpong to Darjeeling, Mary left her family to go with us. Of course, we were very happy to take her and she enjoyed the church services and Bible studies.

God blessed us with wonderful ayahs but we had difficulty finding an honest cook. As a result of British rule, there were many trained cooks but most of them were dishonest and hard to trust. The missionaries would often share stories about their cooks. One missionary had friends over for dinner and when one of them asked, "How does your cook make this tasty clear soup?" she said, "Let's find out." They went into the kitchen and found the cook straining the soup through the missionary's husband's sock. The missionary was horrified and asked, "Why are you using my husband's sock?"

"Oh don't worry, Memsahib, it's not his clean sock."

Another cook was renowned for getting his dumplings into uniform shape. The missionary who had hired him discovered that he took each lump of dough and pressed it into perfect shape under his armpit.

With our cooks, we had to keep things locked up. I suspected our cook was stealing so I peeked into his coat pocket and, sure enough, there was a bag of my sugar. I had to have proof, so I took the sugar that was left on the counter and locked it in the cupboard to see what the cook would say.

He watched me. "Memsahib, what are you doing?"

Frustrated, I said, "Look in your coat pocket and you'll see!"

"Oh Memsahib, you mean the sugar? My wife asked me to buy her some on my way to work. Please ask Mary, she knows."

"I'll ask Mary when she arrives." I waited until the cook left to go home for lunch, feeling sure that he was going to talk to Mary before I could ask her about the sugar. He lived in the opposite direction from Mary, so I watched through the upstairs window to see which direction he would take. When our cook got to the main road, he turned back to check if I was watching him, but he couldn't see me. Then he turned and walked towards Mary's house. When Mary arrived back from her lunch break, she seemed very nervous.

"Did the cook talk to you?" I asked.

"Yes Memsahib, but he told me if I told you, he would hurt me. I'm afraid, so please don't tell him."

"What did he say to you, Mary?"

"He told me to tell you that his wife asked him to buy her some sugar, but Memsahib, I can't tell a lie. He didn't buy that sugar."

"Don't worry Mary, I won't tell him."

I was spared the trouble of confronting the cook because after a few days he quit.

Shortly after this we moved to Darjeeling and Mary came with us as our ayah. We prayed for God to give us an honest cook and we found Sarah who was separated from her husband and had five small children. She was honest, cheerful and a hard worker. Mary taught her about the Bible and Christianity and Sarah became a believer and was baptized. Sarah worked for us for many years and her whole family became Christians.

While we were still in Kalimpong Fern, who was six at the time, came in from the backyard crying because she had hurt her leg. It was just a little scratch, so we put a band-aid on it. During the night, her pain grew worse, so we took her to the doctor in Kalimpong. The doctor couldn't find anything but gave her a tetanus shot. When we arrived in Darjeeling, Fern began to lose control of her leg. Realizing that something was seriously wrong, we walked a mile-and-a-half to the doctor. Fern had to walk too and was in a lot of pain. The doctor, a British woman, was sick at the time but, because it was an emergency, came in. She examined Fern but couldn't figure out what was wrong. Then, as she felt around in the wound, she said, "We need to operate immediately. Bring her in tomorrow morning."

We made Fern walk back home with us, then we walked back to the hospital in the morning. After the operation, the doctor said,

"Look what was in your daughter's leg."

She held up a bamboo stake the size of my little finger. It had gone in the front of Fern's leg and was almost coming out the back.

"It's a miracle gangrene didn't set in," the doctor said.

I began crying, thinking of how much pain my daughter must have been in and how we had made her walk to and from the hospital. We took her back home in a taxi and she healed well although she still has the scar today.

Darjeeling, famous for its tea, is in the Himalayas 6710 ft. above sea level. Darjeeling is either in the clouds or above them and the dampness turned our shoes green with mildew. With 250 inches of rain per year, there were constant deluges. When we walked through the grass, black leeches would cling all over our legs, starting out small then swelling with our blood. They couldn't be pulled off, so we carried a saltshaker to get them off when we finally got to our destination.

After many months we planted a church in North Point, about one-and-a-half miles from Darjeeling. We lived near Mt. Hermon School, which our kids attended. In North Point we lived in Grace Cottage, which was surrounded by heavy woods. We were told that the missionaries that had lived there previously had come into the room one day when their baby was sleeping and a tiger had been perched on the windowsill about to pounce on their baby. We had to be careful, but Tim, who was four, would go into the jungle and brag about having killed a tiger one day and a bear the next, just as if he were as brave as David in the Bible.

Mount Hermon School

The church in North Point grew quickly as God continued to confirm His Word with signs and wonders.

While we were in Darjeeling, our vegetable lady asked us to come to their house and pray for their son. "He's been ill since he was two years old," she said. "We gave the witch doctor twelve chickens and a pig for a sacrifice, but after the sacrifice our son got even worse."

We had seen the boy on several occasions. He was twenty-one but very small for his age. He sat in a corner all day and couldn't walk or talk and had recently stopped eating. He looked like such a hopeless case that we were reluctant to go and pray for him, but his parents kept asking us to come. We prayed and fasted, asking God for wisdom and boldness. Then we went to their home and prayed. Their flea-ridden dog was lying on the floor nearby scratching himself, distracting us during the prayers and Alfred got quite annoyed. After several hours of praying we saw no improvement and went home discouraged.

Soon after we arrived home the boy's father came to us and said, "Please come pray for our dog. Now he has the same problems as our son."

"How is your son?"

"He's well! He's starting to eat again."

We felt encouraged and went back to pray, not for the dog but for the boy. The dog died but the boy was healed. We told the parents that the demons and sickness had left the boy and entered into the dog, just like when Jesus cast out the demons from a man and they entered into a herd of nearby pigs, causing them to run into the lake and drown. The parents were so pleased they became Christians and shared the good news with their neighbours. They named the boy David. He actually grew six inches while we were on furlough and was able to speak. The first word he spoke was "Jesus."

A family in their neighbourhood heard about David and the miracle of healing. They came to our house and asked if they could join us because they had heard God was in our midst. We told them they were welcome to come to our meetings and learn about the miracle-working God. The whole family of eighteen joined the church and became followers of Jesus. The little church grew and now has multiplied to about a hundred churches. All things are possible with God.

A short time after we arrived in Darjeeling, Mary received news that her sister had fallen from a high stack of wool where she worked. She was very ill with internal injuries and wanted Mary to come and visit her. Alfred went with her and they prayed for her sister. While praying, Mary noticed her father's favourite idol sitting on the shelf. She grabbed the idol and threw it on the floor, where it broke into pieces. Mary's father was very upset and refused to talk to her, but her sister was healed and able to return to work.

Seeing Mary's boldness and desire to serve the Lord, we sent her to the same Bible school that Rajani was attending. Mary spent three years there and graduated with honours. She then came back and helped us with a Nepali Bible correspondence school that we had started.

After Mary went to Bible school we met Dinah Mary. She was fifteen years old when she became a Christian and wanted to be baptized.

"You need to get written permission from your mother," we told her, as her father was dead. She did so and we baptized her. When she arrived home after the baptism, her eldest brother was very upset and threw her out of the house, forbidding her to ever come back. When she came to us for refuge, we welcomed her into our home. She helped us with our children, but it was dangerous for her to remain so close to her home and her angry brother, so we decided to send her to Bible school. She was very happy to leave her village and was a good student. After graduating from Bible school, she went into nurse's training.

Fern, Me, Alfred, Ruth Tim, Grace & Dan

In 1959, it was time for us to go home on furlough. We had been in India for six years and now had five children. We traveled by train to Calcutta then flew to England. We didn't have money to get back to Canada so we stayed at the WEC headquarters in England and put the children in school. Finally we got enough money for a booking on the *Queen Elizabeth II*. It only took 5 days to cross the Atlantic to New York.

When we arrived we stayed at the WEC headquarters, until we went on deputation visiting different churches across Canada. We stopped in Winnipeg to visit family and stayed at Helen's place.

I went to visit my sister Emma, but when I knocked on the door I was told, "Didn't you know she died? You just missed the

Back Row: Grace and Daniel
Front Row: Ruth, Timothy and Fern

funeral." I couldn't believe no one had told me.

I also discovered that while we were away, Roy's canoe - the one we had built together that one summer - had been found in a lake, empty. Roy's body was never found. He was only 41 and there was no funeral or memorial. I wanted to talk to the family about this, but by then a few years had passed and they only wanted to forget what had happened.

We continued our journey to Three Hills, Alberta. There was a home for missionary children on furlough, but they didn't have room for our kids so they rented a little place for us nearby. It had two bedrooms, no running water, a wood-burning stove and an outhouse. It was worse than living in India and reminded me of being back on the farm. Still, we were happy to be home and at $25 a month, the rent was cheap. We adjusted to the challenges and spent a whole year there. The kids attended the Three Hills Christian School while we did deputation work. During school holidays we visited family and friends.

My sister Helen had heard our father was ill, so she asked us to go find him and send him to stay with her. Alfred and I went and tracked him down. We found him in a little shack in New Westminster, where he worked in the lumber mill. He was coughing with pneumonia and his shack was filthier than anything we'd seen in India. We put him on the train and sent him to my sister in Winnipeg. He lived with her for awhile, but she was strict about smoking and drinking, so eventually he left.

This is a picture of me and my Dad, John Feuerbach
The photo was taken when I was back for a visit from Bible School. Unfortunately, I do not have any other photos of the two of us together.

Chapter 8
South India

After our furlough was over we returned to India and after about one year in Darjeeling and the surrounding area we moved to Ootacamund, in the hills of South India

1960 Back Row: Grace, Fern, and Daniel
Front Row: Timothy, and Ruth

We lived in a beautiful, big old house called Farley, built by the British. Many years before, C.T. Studd, the founder of WEC, had visited Ooty and spoke at the Union Church, which the owners of Farley attended. They were so impacted by his messages that when they made out their will they decided to give their property to WEC, since they had no family. Because WEC had no workers in Ooty at the time, they placed Farley under the care of a board with several members, designating it for use for God's work. When no longer needed, Farley was to be sold and the money given to WEC. However, the board members were selfish and kept the gift a secret.

Farley Guest House

When the last board member was sick and dying in a hospital in England he became convicted about the property. Wanting to make it right, he called the WEC leader and told him they should send someone to Farley to take possession of the property. WEC sent a missionary couple to check it out and they were amazed to find the beautiful property, complete with a car and a trust fund for operating costs. They began running it as a guest home for WEC missionaries. When they left after a year, WEC sent word to Darjeeling to see if anyone was available to come and take their place. We volunteered and were happy to leave Darjeeling and go south.

Arriving in Farley was like a missionary's dream come true. The house was painted green with a red-tiled roof, surrounded by English gardens and tall eucalyptus trees, with a view of the Nilgiri hills. There was also a tennis court and two cabins on the grounds. We had a big lawn but no lawnmower, so Alfred had to cut all the grass with a knife. We continued running Farley as a guest house and during school breaks we welcomed many families who came from as far as Kashmir.

One day a message came from the girls' boarding school just behind our place asking if Alfred could come and help them get rid of the rock bees that had landed in a swarm by the girls' dorm. Alfred kept bees as a hobby at Farley and was anxious to get the bees for his hive. He took an old pillowcase to capture the bees. While he was pulling the pillowcase over the swarm of bees, some of them crept up his sleeve and stung him. He must have had about eighty stings, which was great cause for concern. Nevertheless he carried the bees home and put them in one of the hives. Then he almost collapsed from the poison in his arm. We contacted the doctor who gave him an antihistamine to help him recover. After a few days he was well and glad to have the new bees.

Often people tried to collect eucalyptus leaves from around our house to build fires with or for making eucalyptus oil. We chased them off the property because we needed the leaves to heat water for our guests. One day while walking around the property, we found some ribbons tied onto the bushes by the path. We knew they were placed there as curses, but we removed them and didn't pay too much attention. At the time we had two cows for milk for the family. Awhile after we found the curses, we went to check the cows and one of them was lying on the ground half-dead. We didn't know what had happened so we called the vet. He told us our cow had been poisoned and gave the cow a double-dose shot of calcium. He warned Alfred to be careful because this would cause the cow to rear up. Sure enough, the cow reared up and started to walk.

Our children attended boarding school while we were in Ooty, which was expensive. The girls stayed at Hebron Girls' School in Conoor, eighteen miles away, while the boys walked to Lushington School for Boys in Ooty. Before they started school, I had to knit and sew most of their clothing and also sew a nametag on each item.

One month we didn't have enough money to pay our bills. We went to the school office to apologise and promised to pay as soon as God provided. The secretary in the office laughed. She handed us a receipt saying an anonymous person in India had paid our school bill in full. This person continued to do so for many months. We never found out who it was.

In Ooty I became pregnant with my sixth child. Fortunately I was  staying close to the hospital and was walking when my waters broke, so I just walked to the hospital. It was the first time Alfred came for the labour and birth. Eunice Joy was born on April 26, 1960. After the birth, I began to hemorrhage. As the nurses came rushing in, Alfred got scared and left the room. They would have given me a transfusion but had no blood bank.

The doctor said, "It's too dangerous for you to have any more children. If you do get pregnant, come in for delivery with someone who has your blood type."

The day after Eunice was born; Alfred brought Ruth in on the scooter. She had shoved a bean into her ear canal and had to have it removed at the hospital. They put her in the same room as me and she stayed overnight, very happy to be with her new sister and me. The next day all the kids came to meet the baby.

Shortly after I came home with Eunice, I went to the school nurse for a check-up. She looked at the baby then looked at me and said, "Edna, you're all yellow – you have jaundice."

The doctor confirmed it and said I'd have to spend six weeks in bed. This was very difficult to follow with a baby and with Ruth, who was only four. Fortunately, Ruth was good at entertaining herself; happily playing in the big yard at Farley and watching people play tennis. She would come and sit beside my bed with the "Dick and Jane" readers, asking me what the words were. Day after day we went over the words until she could read them all.

When the school year started, we felt that Ruth was ready to go to boarding school. We thought that because she had two older sisters in the same school, she'd adjust. We visited Hebron almost every weekend and took the kids home for a weekend every month. When we saw Ruth, she seemed to be doing well. Little did we know that the struggles she had being away from home were memories that would remain with her for a long time. Still, there were good times at boarding school. On Hebron Day all the kids had to dress up and I got very creative with costumes. One year I dressed Ruth up as "co-ed," sewing together half a boys' uniform and half a girls' uniform. She won first prize, which upset the principle because she didn't think the boys' and girls' schools would ever join. It turned out my costume was prophetic, because years later, they did join. I also dressed Grace up as a missionary home on furlough. She had an out-of-style dress, high-heeled shoes, a big purse and her hair in a bun. Fern and another girl went as a dobi's donkey carrying a bundle of dirty clothes. There was also Lushington Day at the boys' school and one year I dressed Tim up as a Native American with a tepee.

From Left to Right: Grace, Al, Eunice, Daniel, Fern, Tim & Ruth

While at Farley, we went to take a vacation by the sea. The kids loved swimming in the water and spending time at the beach. One time when the kids went swimming in the ocean, Fern developed an ear infection that wouldn't clear up. The doctor referred her to

Fern After Surgery

Mysore for surgery, so I drove with her 90 miles on the scooter along winding roads to the Mysore hospital. On the way, we encountered a band of monkeys. Since Hindus worship monkeys, we'd been told, "If you ever hit a monkey in India, step on the gas – don't stop until you reach the nearest police station." So I drove through the crowd of monkeys very carefully. In Mysore the doctor told us operating on the inner ear canal was risky because Fern's face could be paralyzed. If she didn't have the surgery however, the infection might not clear up. I decided to go ahead with the operation and Fern came through without problems.

For another vacation, we decided to take the kids for an elephant ride in the Mysore jungle. We had to get up very early and drive about 50 miles, where we made arrangements for two elephants. The elephants kneeled down so we could climb up onto their backs. On top of the elephants were platforms for us to sit on with our legs dangling over the edge. The guide sat just above the elephant's head, touching its ears with his bare feet to direct it. Two guides with guns walked beside us. While we were going through the thick jungle, one of the guides said, "Be very quiet – there's a rogue elephant on the loose!"

We sat there very quietly, but our elephants made a lot of noise breaking their way through the jungle. The guide told us that several days earlier a rogue elephant had attacked one of their elephants. It was very exciting, but although we saw many other animals, the rogue elephant stayed out of sight.

Tim, Dan, Fern, Grace, Me

An old missionary friend, Miss Boory, came to stay with us at Farley. She had been having severe stomach pains, but when she went to visit the Indian doctors, they hadn't been able to find anything wrong with her and had decided she was simply imagining it. While she was with us, the pain became so bad that we took her to the doctor in Ooty. He told us we needed to take her to the hospital in Mysore for surgery, so we did. When the doctors there opened her up, they discovered she was full of cancer. There was nothing they could do; the cancer had progressed too far and she was dying. Alfred stayed with her at the hospital, where she grew weaker. When it came to the end, Alfred held Miss Boory while our friend Moira sang, "The Lord is my Shepherd," until Miss Boory passed away. Her family didn't respond when we tried to contact them, so we buried her in Mysore and I inherited all her clothes. One of the dresses became one of Ruth's favourites and she wore it even when she had children of her own.

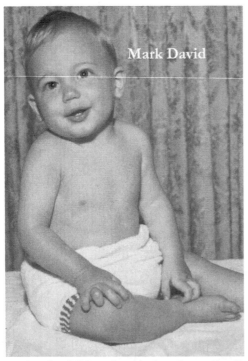

Mark David

While at Farley, Alfred and I talked about what the doctor had said when I gave birth to Eunice. We decided to trust God to protect me if I became pregnant again. So after five years I conceived my seventh child. When I had to go to the hospital, Mrs. Shaw, a friend who had the same blood type came along to the hospital with me, in case I needed a blood transfusion. However, the birth went smoothly and after my shortest labour ever, I delivered Mark on October 10, 1965. He was a miracle child and completed our family.

After eleven years in India, we felt it was time to go back to Canada. Just before we left for Canada, Mary Lata met a young pastor and they got married. They pastored a church in Madras for many years and God blessed them with two wonderful children.

My time in India reminds me of the words of an old hymn:

Great is Thy faithfulness;
Great is Thy faithfulness;
Morning by morning, new mercies I see;
All I have needed,
Thy hand hath provided;
Great is Thy faithfulness, Lord unto me.

God is faithful. Although we started out from Beamsville with no support at all, during our years in India we never lacked anything. We always had enough money to support ourselves, help other missionaries and send young people to Bible school. More than the money, we had also seen God work the miraculous and bring many people to know Him.

Here I am with some of my Sunday school students.

Chapter 9
Return to Canada

After praying about leaving, Alfred and Daniel felt that we would be home in time for Christmas 1965. We heard about a ship that was leaving India for Italy in December and was offering fare at half price. It was a miracle we had learned about it at all, since it had secretly come to India to get the Indian ambassador back home from Pakistan because of conflict between the two countries. We called the shipping company for information and they told us if we could be in Bombay in two weeks we could sail with them to Italy. We sent them a small down payment even though we didn't have all the money for the fare. Even at half price, it was a lot for a family of nine, so we prayed and told God how much we needed. This was a great challenge to our faith. Would God supply? We had no choice but to trust Him. We sold whatever we couldn't take home: books, pots, pans and our scooter. Money started to come in from other missionaries and complete strangers. At last we had enough money for our trip to Italy, but not for our trip to New York. We kept trusting that God would provide.

Time was short and we had to get all our international injections before we could leave India. I took all seven kids to the clinic for the shots.

"The chief medical officer is on holiday," the secretary told me. "Only he can sign the certificates."

"But our train is leaving Ooty tonight! Please help us. Isn't there anyone else who can sign them?"

"Yes, there's one other person, but he lives across town. If you can get his signature before five o' clock, we'll give you the injections."

I hurried across town and walked straight into the office. In India, you always need an appointment first and nothing ever goes according to plan. Knowing it could take days to get the certificates signed, I was desperate and didn't care about protocol.

I went up to the officer and pushed the certificates towards him, "My family and I have to leave Ooty on a train tonight for Bombay. If we don't catch that train, we'll miss our boat to get back to

Canada. I need you to sign these forms so we can get the injections we need before we leave."

To my amazement, he signed them without any questions. I went back to the other office where the children were waiting. It was almost five o' clock, but they gave us the injections.

We made our train that night, with everyone excited to be on our way. Mark was only six weeks old. Since there were no disposable diapers available, I ripped up old towels and made my own diapers. On the train, we threw them out the window. At one stop a boy saw me throw one out the window. He picked it up and ran after the train calling,

"Memsahib, you lost a towel!"

"Thank you," I said, taking the towel from him but feeling very embarrassed.

It took us three days to get to Bombay. As always, we rode third class, unreserved, the train overcrowded as Indian trains always are. Although it was difficult with seven children, we all rode together and didn't have to transfer as often as our first train trip in India. Also, we had the older children to help with the younger ones. We arrived in Bombay without losing any of the kids and were able to get rid of all those dirty home-made diapers.

Soon we were on our way to Italy. The ship was a floating school, an organization in England used it to take school kids on tours to different international sites. We had eight bunk beds in our room and were glad we could all be together. After a few days a big storm arose and everyone was seasick, even the chief steward.

As we piled up the bags of vomit, we joked, "Look at all our Christmas presents!"

The storm kept getting worse and we became desperate. One morning we read the story of how the apostle Paul was in a great storm. He prayed and God calmed the storm. We realized we were on the Mediterranean Sea where Paul had been, so we prayed and asked God to calm the storm. The sea became calm and we had a good voyage the rest of the way to Italy.

We reached our hotel after midnight and were greeted with a big meal, including a roast pig with an apple in its mouth. We were too tired to enjoy the meal and just wanted to go to bed. After a few days we received word saying the money for our fare had arrived.

We boarded the plane and were on our way to New York. Everyone enjoyed the plane ride, even baby Mark slept all the way from Italy to New York.

We arrived in New York several days before Christmas. The first night it snowed. Some of our kids had never seen snow and were up early the next morning playing in the snow in their pyjamas. We spent Christmas in Philadelphia at the WEC international headquarters. After Christmas we left for Canada. Because five of our children were born in India, they didn't have Canadian passports. After being delayed for hours at the border, we were finally allowed to cross into Canada. We stayed in Beamsville and enrolled the children in school. They found the adjustment difficult. In India they had attended a school with British curriculum and had all worn school uniforms. Fern wrote about her feelings on returning to Canada.

Returning to Canada from India as a 14-year-old was very tough. The love in the family was not enough, as I so badly wanted to be accepted by those in my age group. I felt poor, unfashionable and awkward. High school was a terrifying experience every single day, with the crowded halls and the unfamiliar presence of boys in the classroom. Worse, I never understood what anyone was talking about.

Everything was strange - the music, movies, slang, fashion. All through my first year in Canada I kept quiet and desperately observed what was going on around me. Even eating was a problem, because the British way was keeping the knife in the right hand and the fork in the left hand at all times, squashing peas and vegetables onto the backside of the fork with the knife. In Canada, people cut the food with the knife and fork like the British but then lay down the knife and transfer the fork to the right hand, sometimes using the knife to push food onto the inside of the fork. It doesn't seem important now but, at the time, I wanted to blend in and not attract attention to my foreignness. I never let anyone know that I had lived in India for the same reason.

There were some fun times. I remember wearing my new white go-go boots on the snowy sidewalk. For once I felt stylish and normal. Watching others sliding joyfully on the ice, I tried too and fell hard on my backside in mortal embarrassment.

After a few months of adjusting to life in North America, it was time to go on the dreaded deputation tour, where missionaries must visit all the churches that support them. The children are paraded in cute ethnic costumes in front of the church and they have to sing songs in lovely foreign languages, spending each night in a different home where they can feel the resentment of the host children who are required to play with the visiting kids. Then the next day would be another day of traveling in a cramped car with grumpy siblings, getting bored and carsick and doing it all over again. I refused. My parents realized that life would be unbearable for all of us if they forced me to come along. So I was allowed to stay with my friend for the summer and keep an eye on my baby brother.

Thank God I always had one good friend wherever we went. That probably saved my life. I was so grateful for any kindness or acceptance, but it never lasted long. Each time I started to feel comfortable, we were ripped away into a new town, new school, new church. Of course, our family became our most stable community and we were always able to rely on each other for companionship in a game of Monopoly or Rook.

It probably sounds as if I am bitter about this part of my life. However, I actually do not regret any of these experiences. I realize that I am able to adapt to new situations and I also have great compassion for those who are on the margins of society. I am drawn to the immigrants, disabled and poor people and anyone I notice who doesn't fit in. I chose a job where I can hang out with immigrants and refugees all day and I think I can help them better because I understand them a little.

So, thanks Mom and Dad. I believe I have had a rich life. I watched the way your faith in God motivated and strengthened you. You loved me and taught me and inspired me. I also realized later that all 14 year-olds have a terrible year as they adjust to their own new country of adulthood. So I am okay with all of it now. I love you.

We stayed in Beamsville until the end of the school year. Just before leaving, I had a miscarriage. We also received word that Alfred's father was very sick and not expected to live much longer. Everything was happening very fast and Alfred wanted to see his dad before he passed away. I was still feeling weak and depressed from losing a baby and wasn't looking forward to traveling for days in a small car with seven children. Fern decided to stay in Beamsville. A friend of WEC offered to take care of Mark, who was only six months old. After much prayer and discussion, we decided to leave Mark with this friend. It would make it easier to travel and leave more room for the rest of us in the small car. We packed our things in the car and headed out west.

We arrived at the hospital and spent some time with Alfred's father. Alfred was able to share and pray with him and after he passed away we attended the funeral. Then we traveled on to British Columbia, where we stayed with friends and Alfred's brother Herald until we were able to get our own place. Eventually, God provided us with a small farm and an old house in Rosedale, which we moved into without any furniture. That night, people came with beds, food and everything else we needed for the night. The next day more things arrived and we were amazed at how God provided for our family.

As soon as we were settled, Alfred drove back to Ontario to pick up Mark and Fern. When they came home, I reached out to take Mark from Fern. He drew back from me and I suddenly realized he didn't know who I was. I felt terrible for leaving him without me for so long. For weeks he was afraid to be left alone, so I took him to the raspberry field where he would climb onto my back while I weeded and hoed. I've repented many times and asked for forgiveness for leaving him alone.

The small farm didn't provide us with enough income, so Alfred found a job. After about six months on the farm, we bought a larger, eleven-acre raspberry farm in Yarrow. We had no experience with raspberries, but were willing to work hard and learn. Since Alfred was away most of the day working, the farm was my responsibility. After the children came home from school, they would put down their books, grab a hoe and work until supper time without complaining

We somehow managed to take care of the farm, but there was little rain the first year so the crop was poor. Alfred was working full-time building fireplaces so we managed to make ends meet. The next year just before harvest, Alfred became very ill and had major surgery on both kidneys. He spent six weeks in the hospital. The kids and I had to carry on with the farm with no income until harvest time. Somehow with everyone's hard work and God's help we survived. We stayed on the farm for three years and the last year we had a bumper crop of raspberries which allowed us to buy a new station wagon.

Daniel talks about the raspberry farm.

We had a raspberry farm in Yarrow, BC for several years and I remember going along with my mom to the raspberry co-op shortly after we had sold the farm. If the market price for raspberries was good, then the co-op would distribute a bonus to the growers at the end of the season. There was a bonus that year and Mom insisted that we got our share. Eventually the manager agreed and said, "Guess that's the easiest thousand dollars you ever got." Mom answered without missing a beat, "Easy? We earned it all through last year when we pruned and hoed and then picked the berries!" This is a typical example of how she stood her ground until her insistence paid off, but her boldness often embarrassed me when I was young.

Sometime later I got a call saying my father had passed away in Winnipeg. I really didn't have a relationship with him, but I felt obligated to go to his funeral for my family's sake. I took a train headed to Winnipeg, but halfway to Edmonton there was a snow slide and the train couldn't continue. I had to take a bus to Edmonton then a plane to Winnipeg. I arrived just in time for the funeral. It was a typical three-day Ukrainian funeral with a lot of drinking, which made me feel out of place. I'd fulfilled my obligation and was anxious to get home to be with my family.

Chapter 10
The House of Prayer

After three years, we sold the raspberry farm and were ready for our next adventure. This was the beginning of our many moves, sixty in just thirty-eight years. This way of life was very hard on all of us, but especially on our kids once they became teenagers.

After a year in Kelowna waiting for our visa to go and pastor a church in Illinois, the church found another pastor so we moved to Abbotsford, where Alfred continued to work building fireplaces. In Abbotsford, we began hearing about a radical group of Christians called "The Jesus People" who had spread up from California into Vancouver. We were curious to get to know them, wondering if anything good could come out of California since we had only heard of Hollywood and drive-by shootings.

One day I received a call from a Christian friend, asking if I would prepare an Indian meal for a Jesus People retreat near Abbotsford. I agreed and my family and I soon met the Jesus People - about 50 of them. They looked like people from another planet with their long hair, torn jeans and bare feet. I really wanted to get to know them, so after the retreat, we had a group of about 10 or 15 over to our house for lunch. They were hungry and ate lots of food, especially ice cream. We were impressed with their enthusiasm for God. Our kids enjoyed hearing their stories and they began dropping by quite often.

Later on, the Jesus People were invited to hold meetings in the high school gym in Abbotsford. Every evening the meetings were packed with all kinds of people curious about what they'd been hearing. All the Jesus People got onstage together to sing and play with great enthusiasm. They shared exciting testimonies about how they'd come out of drug abuse and other serious situations. The meetings continued for over a week as the local young people, both churched and un-churched, became very interested in what was going on. Some of the parents and pastors were worried about their young people being influenced by the Jesus People's lifestyle, although the Jesus People weren't involved in the drug use and sexual immorality that accompanied the hippy movement they appeared to be part of.

The Jesus People attracted many hippies in Canada as well as draft-dodgers from the US. They believed in using the early church as their model, living in communal houses and keeping "all things in common." In Vancouver, they also had a coffee house called "The Shepherd's Call" where they brought in street people and gathered for worship meetings. Shortly after meeting the Jesus People, we became involved with St. Margaret's church in Vancouver. It had started out as a conservative Episcopalian church, but as it began to welcome the Jesus People, it became more evangelical and a pioneer in the charismatic movement.

At the same time as the Jesus People were growing in Vancouver, a group called the Children of God (COG) was emerging in California and word of them had spread up the west coast. They had gained a strong reputation both for being against the mainstream church and because they were "on-fire" and never lost any of their converts. Russell Griggs, who had brought the Jesus People movement into Canada, was impressed with what he had heard about them and believed that the Jesus People Army could learn from their discipline and dedication. He invited some of them to Vancouver to share little realizing that the Children of God would soon take control.

In Abbotsford, there was a ranch near the border that had previously been an abortion clinic. Originally rented to the Jesus People, it was soon taken over by the Children of God. We visited the ranch a few times and were impressed with their enthusiasm, thinking this group was just another branch of the Jesus People. We began making plans to move into a commune in Vancouver. Our son Tim, who was fifteen at the time, began going to meetings and was very enthusiastic about what they were doing.

One day while we were at the ranch, Alfred overheard some of the COG talking about building a tunnel under the border so they could bring other COG members into Canada illegally. He also heard them talking about guns. We realized that something wasn't right and began to question our plans to join the commune. We told Russell Griggs what we'd heard, but he wasn't convinced and he and many of the other leaders of the Jesus People went to Texas to take their training. While he was gone, the Children of God completed their takeover of the Jesus People.

At this time, Fern and three friends took a road trip and were in California. When their car broke down in the middle of the night some of the Jesus People rescued them, taking them to stay at their commune.

While there, Fern told them, "My parents are planning to join the COG."

Alarmed, they said, "Get on that phone right now and warn your parents not to go in. The COG is a cult."

They told her what had happened in California: how believers had been sucked in and were now unable to escape. Fern called us and we felt this was a confirmation not to join the COG. However, we didn't want to tell the COG we'd decided not to join, because Tim had become deeply involved with them. He had been living in a Jesus People commune when the Children of God had taken over and we were concerned about what might happen to him.

We had to be careful so we told him, "We want you to come home for a few days."

He said, "No, I don't want to."

"Come home and we'll pray with you," we insisted. "Then if you still want to go back you can."

The COG let us take him home because they thought we were still moving into the commune. Tim felt he had been tricked by us and once at home he was very angry and would quote scriptures at us. We fasted and prayed, wondering how we could convince Tim to leave the commune for good. Then one of our friends from the Jesus People became very uncomfortable with what was happening with the COG. He was able to sneak out of the commune to a payphone and call us, asking us to come and get him. We went to pick him up and took him home. As he talked to Tim, Tim began to realize he needed to get out of the COG as well.

However, all of Tim's things were still in the commune. We knew the times when the COG would meet, so we arrived at the commune when we knew they'd all be at the meeting. Tim ran up to his house, climbed through the window and carried out his and his friends' things. Shortly after this, the COG came to our house with a moving truck to help move us to the commune.

"We've changed our minds," we told them. "We don't want to move." They were very upset about this.

At this time, we contacted Pastor Bob Birch of St. Margaret's Church in Vancouver, who had decided to open his church to street kids. He asked us to come and help, saying he would provide a house for us if we wanted to work with these people. We had never been to his church before, so the next Sunday morning we went to check it out. Some of the family felt uncomfortable with the church and we were unsure whether we should move ahead. In the afternoon, we were scheduled to meet with the St. Margaret's elders. The church had begun a ministry among street kids and after meeting with us they asked us to pray with them after the evening service. We did so and they felt confirmation that we were to work with them.

When we agreed to this, the elders purchased a house in Vancouver for us so we could provide a home for new converts and street kids. Arriving with all our things, we found that the deal for the house had fallen through, so we moved into a little apartment, which we shared with a couple of girls from the church. It was cramped and miserable. Thankfully, a couple days later the deal was on again.

We soon moved in with about twenty young people and named our new home "The House of Prayer." Some were already involved with St Margaret's and others were former Jesus People that had been rescued from the COG. Alfred and the Christian young people went to the streets, parks and beaches - wherever young people gathered or hung out - to evangelize. Anyone interested was invited back to the House of Prayer where we provided meals and a place to stay. We also told them that God loved them and had a plan for their lives.

None of the young people who stayed with us had any money and we wouldn't allow them to accept money from welfare. Instead, we had to trust God to supply all our needs. We believed that what God had done in India he could do on the streets of Vancouver. Soon our house was overflowing with young people and we wondered what our neighbors were thinking, seeing so many hippies hanging around.

House of Prayer Group

We didn't have to wait very long to find out. A neighbor from across the street came over and knocked on the door. Reluctantly, I opened the door to hear what she had to say.

She said, "I've noticed lots of young people hanging around your house and I wonder if you could use some extra food. I work at a frozen food plant in Richmond we get a lot of food with wrong and outdated labels. Could we give it to you?"

"Yes, thank you," I said. "We can always use extra food."

"Alright, I'll send some over."

A few days later a truck arrived loaded with all kinds of food. We piled the food on our large table and gathered around it, joining hands to sing, 'Praise God From Whom All Blessings Flow.' Looking around, I could see that everyone in the room had tears in their eyes.

Most of the food was frozen, but we had no freezer to keep it in. We had to buy one as well as borrow space in some of our friends'. As Alfred would say, "God's shovel is bigger than ours - the more we shovel out, the more He shovels in." One time Alfred took twelve small loaves of bread to a Bible school in need of food. The next day we received 200 big loaves of bread. It seemed like the miracle of the loaves and fishes.

We always left our door unlocked and many times we would wake up in the morning and there would be new kids sleeping on the floor in their sleeping bags. Christians from many different churches would pick up hitchhikers and drop them off at our place, night or day. Young girls who ran away from home would end up in our house. People who escaped from The Children of God kept calling and asking us to rescue them, as they had nowhere else to go.

Although many of these young people had come out of serious addictions, we seldom encountered problems with drug use or violent behavior in our house. When they arrived, we prayed against the strongholds of addiction and many were set free. We always asked the young people to contact their parents and let them know where they were staying. Often concerned parents, who had heard about cults in the area, would come to visit and see what kind of a home their children were staying in. They were impressed with how we ran the house and thanked us for helping their kids. Some would even give us money to buy food.

However, not everyone was happy about these changed lives. One evening we were having Bible study when we heard a strange noise coming from outside our house. When Alfred went outside to check where it was coming from, he saw a stranger running away with a gas can in his hand. Sometime later, we received a letter from this man. He wrote that he was upset with us because his girlfriend, who was a witch, had become a Christian and stayed at the House of Prayer. He had come to burn our house down and was ready to light the gasoline he had spread around it, when Alfred had gone outside and scared him away. He had then gone to Winnipeg and stayed in a house like ours, where he had become a Christian. He was writing to ask for our forgiveness.

One evening I was at home while everyone was at church when a knock came at the door. When I opened the door I found a young man there who was breathing heavily. He told me he was doing drugs when he felt the urge to get out of the house and go to a nearby church for help. When he got to the church there was a choir practice going on so he kept running down the street, desperate for help. As he ran, he was listening to a transistor radio and heard about a Christian rock concert. They mentioned the House of Prayer as a place to get more information about it, so he had come to ask if we could give him any details. I invited him in and told him to wait until everyone else came home. We discovered that the concert had already taken place, but he decided to stay with us and soon became a Christian.

When Fern came back from California, she'd been in the Jesus People commune for at least three months. There they were all new at cooking, so they prayed about everything.

One day I was adding some salt to the food and Fern said,

"Mom, you didn't pray about how much salt to put in!"

"Oh Fern, I just used my common sense," I said.

Fern welcomed the young people to come into the kitchen and they would sit on the counters, playing guitar and singing.

I'd get frustrated trying to maneuver around them and would say, "Okay, everyone out of the kitchen!"

Because there was no lock, I'd shove a knife in the door to keep it shut. Sometimes I'd go to the bedroom to get some peace and find Alfred inside counseling several people.

Soon we outgrew the first house, so we rented a larger one in the Shaughnessy area and moved in with about fifty people. We called it the House of Bethel. At Christmas time we would drive around and pick up kids that had nowhere to go and would give them a turkey dinner with all the trimmings. Now we had a counseling room and a larger kitchen for them to hang out in. Some of the young people had been involved in demon worship and needed deliverance from evil spirits. Our experience in India prepared us for this ministry. Alfred was very bold when praying for these kids with demonic spirits. He would get angry with the demons and rebuke them in Jesus' name and they would leave. When these young people became Christians, their lifestyle changed dramatically. Instead of doing drugs and stealing, they now wanted to make restitution and pay back what they had stolen.

While I was at the House of Bethel, I was battling with fear of the dark and staying home alone. Although there were many people in the house, whenever Al was gone I would worry and become anxious, scenes of what might happen kept running through my head. Knowing I had inherited this fear from my mother, I kept praying, "God, set me free from the torment of fear."

House of Bethel

One evening, Alfred had to go to pick up food from a wholesale place. I went to bed alone and the fear hit me suddenly. Paralyzed, I was afraid to pray because it seemed I would be overwhelmed by darkness. Suddenly, I felt myself become a spectator watching myself and I was able to rebuke the fear in boldness. When I returned to myself, I was able to go to sleep. The next day, when I was having a nap on the couch, I had a vision. I was lifted off the couch where I was lying and saw myself seated on top of an Indian elephant. Underneath the elephant, there were all kinds of small ants scattered and running for cover.

As the elephant jolted me high above the ground, I directed it to step on the ants. "There's one – get it!"

Then I remembered a joke I heard in India: "Why does an elephant have ripples under his feet? To give the ants a 50/50 chance!" I laughed, then thought about the possibility of 50% of the ants escaping and was concerned. Then I heard a loud noise behind me. I turned around and saw a huge bulldozer with a large blade scraping up the dirt with the ants that had escaped the elephant's feet. The picture of me on the elephant and the bulldozer behind me getting those tiny ants overwhelmed me.

God showed me that the ants were my fears. My prayers from the night before had slain the mother ant and now the baby ants were scurrying about without their mother. The elephant and the bulldozer had killed all those little ants; now that the mother ant was dead, there would be no more baby ants. I had at last overcome my fears. I was so elated by this revelation that I shared my vision the following day in church. From then on I was nicknamed "Edna the Bulldozer." I had planned to write a book called, "I Am an Over-comer," but I was too busy with other things.

Roger Rayner, one of the men from the House of Prayer shared his testimony with me.

Where does one start in describing the long and winding road that led to the House of Prayer?

I had mysterious experiences and a yearning for God from my earliest childhood but my home life was very trying. I left home at eighteen and found a good job with a computer company in Toronto. At the same time I was drawn to the hippie movement and found myself part of a dubious dichotomy: straight during the week, but attending rock concerts, smoking grass and tripping on weekends

After four years of trying to fit in, I could not find sufficient reality in the cultural norms of a fiancé, furnished apartment and flourishing career. I got rid of my possessions and headed for the road, like a rolling stone with no direction or home, full of emptiness, yet knowing there must be more.

I eventually settled in a rural Buddhist commune in Northern Canada. One day, in frustration, the head monk exclaimed to all, "What's the matter with you, O ye of little faith?" Hmm, a Buddhist monk quoting a scripture that I had heard in Sunday school? When the going gets rough, he turns to the Bible? It was a bit of cognitive dissonance for a budding Buddhist.

From there I went down to Mexico, California, and wherever else, asking questions, seeking, reflecting, tripping. There were spiels and meals at Hare Krishna temples, and arguing with Jesus freaks at Berkeley. While I was marching in an anti-Vietnam war demonstration in San Francisco, some Jesus People were yelling from a third story apartment balcony, "No, no, that's not the way, Jesus is the way!" A friend marching with us exclaimed, "You know, they're right!"

Back to Vancouver I went, then across the prairies, picking up every hippie hitchhiker to help pay for gas. I returned to Toronto briefly. While there, I smoked some very potent hash and started hallucinating uncomfortably. I wandered around, ending up at a Jesus People house, where they prayed for me and brought me down. I didn't accept Christ but mentioned I was moving to Vancouver. They told me I needed to go to St. Margaret's Church, where I would have a wonderful experience.

Arriving in Vancouver in January 1972, I rented an apartment. Upstairs lived a former revolutionary who started telling me about Jesus. When I was walking on the streets, Jesus People would come up to me and talk about Jesus or hand me tracts. I wondered if there was a conspiracy by God to harass me.

One Sunday when I was hitchhiking, a couple picked me up and started talking. Wouldn't you know, it was about Jesus. I mentioned that when I was in Toronto I was told I should go to St. Margaret's Church. To my surprise, they said they were on their way to the church. I walked into the church, seeing wall-to-wall people – hippies, businessmen, old ladies – worshipping. They were singing in an unknown tongue that was so hauntingly beautiful, something that I seemed to have heard in my dreams, but at the same time scary. I was torn, wanting more but also wanting to run out.

The following week, I was arguing with the Jesus Person who lived in the apartment above me. He was presenting Jesus while I was presenting my eclectic mish-mash of Buddhism, the revolution and New Age philosophy. Finally, he banged his fist on the table and pointed right at me: "Look - you either want Jesus or you don't – what do you want?" To my surprise, I answered, "I want Jesus." He said that I needed to go to a prayer meeting, and wrote down the address of a place called "The House of Prayer."

I took a bus to the stop I thought was nearest to the House of Prayer. The ride was very difficult as I was hallucinating and feeling suicidal by this time. I walked down a dark street, trying to find the house but could not. I was about to turn back when I noticed a lady walking on the other side of the street. I walked over to her, asking if she had ever heard of the House of Prayer. To my surprise, she was carrying a large Bible, and replied, "Yes, I'm going there right now." So I accompanied her to the meeting and found a chair. Everyone was very warm and welcoming.

I don't remember a lot about the meeting as I was shaking all over, wondering what was going on inside of me. I was doing addition in my head, 2+2=4, etc., concluding that I was still rational. Pastor Birch gave a brief message and said that he had to leave early. As he went out the door, I ran out after him into the pouring rain. I told him I had to talk with him because I was shaking all over. He invited me into his car. There he shared the Gospel with me. I told him that was too good to be true, that I had messed up my life too much. With that, he pointed his finger at me and proclaimed sternly, "Satan, I rebuke you in Jesus' name!" I felt myself thrown up against the car door and then I began to weep profusely from my gut. I hadn't cried in years but something happened in that moment as he led me in prayer to receive Christ on February 10, 1972 around 8:30 at night.

Pastor Birch had to leave so I went back into the House of Prayer. Right away, some of the young people looked at me and said, "You've accepted Christ, haven't you? Your face is different..." I said yes, and they all congratulated me, inviting me back to their meetings.

At the House of Prayer, I got to know Pastor Al Adam, who agreed that I could move there to be further discipled. The moment I had accepted Christ, I immediately felt called into ministry, whatever that meant, so I left my apartment and moved into the House of Prayer's men's house. Al took me under his wing as a son. I often accompanied him to wash floors at grocery stores that would donate day-old food for our janitorial services, or pick up loads of donated bread with him. Once we swapped a load of bread with the John Howard Society in exchange for a load of Carnation Instant Breakfast. Al and I talked a lot together (probably taking too much of his time from his family) and I felt very close to him. I was so hungry about the things of the Lord and wanted to know so much. Finally I had found the reason for which I was created.

Al's son Tim became a dear friend. Although Tim was several years younger than me, and sometimes shy, he knew the Scriptures and was able to answer a lot of my questions. I could relate easily to his contemplative nature. I tease Tim today that if I'm off track in my spiritual walk, it's because I was his disciple!

At the House of Prayer we would have breakfast, daily devotions and Bible study, household duties and witnessing outreaches on a daily basis. In the midst of this invasion of young people needing spiritual parents, it was a constant challenge for Edna to keep the house in order, arrange meals, assign chores and try to mother her own family. Her sacrifices are greatly appreciated.

Almost everyone played a guitar, so I gradually picked up the chords of the many favorite choruses. We would go on many outreaches, whether downtown, to UBC or wherever. I would often bring back the homeless looking for a meal, until Pastor Al finally counseled me that the Salvation Army was better set up for alcoholics – the House of Prayer mandate was to reach young people. We would all pile into the van for services at St. Margaret's, picking up unsuspecting hitchhikers and wondering what God would do that day, as the air was often electric with expectancy.

Needless to say, there are many, many stories that I could tell from the time of my spiritual formation at the House of Prayer. I stayed there from February to December, 1972 before returning east, eventually going to Bible College and into ministry full-time, first pastoring then church-planting, administration/communications, and now as an inter-denominational pastoral/ prayer counselor, which is only fitting for a graduate of the House of Prayer!

My Christian walk since the House of Prayer has taken many twists and turns through the challenges of life, not to mention the distinct peculiarities of church involvement. However, the basics of simple faith, prayer and meaningful fellowship that were developed at the House of Prayer have remained. My loving wife Sheila has appreciated getting to know my spiritual roots and the friendships that have so deeply transformed my life.

Al and Edna Adam welcomed me into their family at the House of Prayer. They and their children were a joy and so kind to me. I am sure the endless stream of needy young people coming and going must have put a tremendous strain on their whole family. I am eternally grateful that at a major crossroads in my life, in very tumultuous times, I found a safe and soft place to land at the House of Prayer. Only eternity will reveal how many lives have been touched through such a sacrificial ministry *demonstrating the love of God to a generation of lost young people. Thank you, Jesus! Thank you, Al and Edna. Thank you Tim, Dan, Fern, Grace, Ruth, Eunice, and Mark. You are special people!*

Chapter 11
Time for a Change

After two years of working with street kids, we needed a change. Although we were blessed by seeing so many kids come to the Lord, the work was hard on the family. Since space was limited the kids had to share their rooms. We were always caring for large numbers of people and were involved in intense spiritual warfare and counselling. It was time for us to take a break and move onto something new. We decided to move to Campbell River on Vancouver Island, where we had friends who'd invited us to join them.

After we left, we often wondered what had become of all the young people that passed through the House of Prayer. Twenty-five years later, Daniel and Fern organized a reunion. Many of those kids, who were now adults, shared amazing stories of what had happened since they left the House of Prayer. Some had become pastors while others took training and pursued different careers. I wept hearing their testimonies, knowing it was worth all the hard work. I'd gladly do it all over again.

At the House of Bethel, we had had a lease for $1,700 a month but we wanted to leave before the lease ended. The owner had a potential buyer so we both signed an agreement to break the lease. Then the potential buyer backed out and the owner wanted us to keep the lease, but we were already moving to Campbell River so we left. After living in Campbell River for about a month, we heard a commotion outside our house at night. We looked out and saw a tow truck hooking up our Toyota car to take it away. Our car was collateral on the lease. We didn't know what to do, so we called a Christian lawyer friend, Al Lazerte. He drove the two miles to our place and confronted the men who had come to tow our car. "Get this tow truck off the yard and get off this property or I'll see you in court."

They left but Al said, "They'll be back. If I were you I'd hide your cars for awhile."

We took our station wagon and the Toyota and hid them on a friend's property, then borrowed another car. After a month or so Al told us it would be okay to take our cars out of hiding. A little while later, we were at a church service and Tim wasn't feeling well so he went to sleep in the Toyota. He heard a rumbling and sat up - there was a tow truck about to tow away the car. Tim ran into church and told us, "There's a tow truck taking away our car!"

Al Lazert was at church too, so we all rushed outside together. The landlord had brought his lawyer and after talking to her, Al Lazerte eventually said there was nothing he could do. They left us the station wagon and took the new Toyota to put in storage in Vancouver until the court case. Al Lazerte said he thought it was better we leave them with the car than go to court, since it would cost us less to lose the car. We never saw the Toyota again.

Campbell River was experiencing a revival in the mainstream churches. My friend Betsy Foort was touched by the Spirit in the Catholic Church and started Bible studies at her home where the Spirit touched many of her friends. She needed help with the Bible studies so she asked me to join her. Home meetings sprung up all over, including one at Al Lazerte's that we also helped with. People came from all around the surrounding area, many staying until midnight to talk and pray. Later Betsy's husband Lawrence, who hadn't been interested in church, began attending the Baptist church.

My friends, Debbie and Kip McMurchie were attending the Lutheran church and touched by the Spirit.

Debbie shared her story with me.

It was a chilly, rainy night at the Adam's house in Campbell River. Betsy, Edna and I were sitting around the kitchen table with my nine-month old son, David. We were having a fine visit and a cup of tea. It was bedtime for David and since Edna was an extraordinary mother with seven kids to her credit, she elected to do the honors and put him to sleep in her room. David adored her and she had accomplished this task many times before. Unfortunately this particular night her magic didn't seem to work. He just wouldn't settle. However Edna, to her credit, persevered. Just when she thought he was asleep, she'd come into the other room and he'd wake up again.

The last time, she was gone for so long I went in the check on them. There was Edna kneeling beside the bed patting him my son on the back, gently soothing him to sleep. It looked like she was finally winning with the sleepy little guy. I went back out to the kitchen. I knew Edna would be back with us soon.

As we sipped our tea and chatted we looked up to see Edna sneaking quietly out of the bedroom door and crawling on her hands and knees down the hallway. We took a second look and there was little David crawling quietly behind her with a big smile ear-to-ear, proud as punch and responding to our gales of laughter. I can still see the puzzled look on Edna's face as she looked behind her to see what all the hilarity was about. When she saw him she crumpled in fits of giggles and laughter, scooped him up and gave him a big hug. I can't remember if he ever did go to sleep that night, but it didn't seem to matter because I have never laughed so hard in my life.

Sunday afternoons were spent at the Adam's house after church. There could be anywhere from twelve to 50 people in attendance. Everyone contributed something. Kids played in the large yard and parents visited. This was something Edna and Al contributed to every place they lived in. Their example is a large part of my commitment to community in my own life today. We all looked forward to those gatherings.

I remember being in charge of bringing the buns. I would spend a good part of my Saturday baking buns from scratch. When it came to packaging them up to take over to Edna's I would want to keep some of them for my family. My attitude wasn't one of true generosity. I remember sharing this with Edna. Her suggestion was that every time I wanted to withhold I should put another bun in the bag. It only took a couple of weeks and lots of extra buns but I was able to quell that nasty little greedy voice once and for all. I have used this advice over and over in my life with great success. Thanks Edna.

It was wonderful times of seeing God move in a new way in the mainstream churches.

Despite the revival, we also went through intense spiritual struggles at the time. We were living with Al Lazerte for a while and Tim was leading worship at his home meeting. One day, Tim told us he had decided to no longer be a Christian. We spent some time discussing the reasons for his decision.

At one point he said, "Mom, you almost persuade me to change my mind, but I can't turn back. I've made up my mind. I've decided to leave home, because it wouldn't be fair to stay here and not go to church or help with the home meeting."

I was heartbroken. I couldn't understand why God would allow this to happen and wondered where we had failed as parents. I even began to question God's reality and Jesus' sacrifice for my sins. "Is Christianity a myth?" I wondered. I was bombarded with torment and couldn't pray. I'd never before doubted my salvation or faith in God. Now I couldn't shake the doubts. I felt I was going through the same struggle as Tim was. I went to bed but couldn't sleep. I turned to Alfred. "Alfred, I need you to pray for me."

He prayed and took authority over the attacks, rebuking Satan and pleading the blood of Jesus. Still the doubts and torment remained. Then a verse of Scripture came into my mind, 2 Cor. 11:3: "But I fear, lest somehow, as the serpent deceived Eve by craftiness, so your minds may by corrupted from the simplicity that is in Christ." As I meditated on that verse, peace began to fill my mind and the torment was gone. God showed me that Tim no longer believed in the simplicity that is in Christ. Now Satan was attacking my mind and causing all these doubts to try and lead me away from my faith in Jesus. I realized that if I'd experienced some of what Tim was suffering, I could understand why he'd decided to leave the faith. I decided to intercede for him.

One evening after our home meeting, Tim came upstairs for the snacks we always served our guests. He had been downstairs in his room while the meeting was going on upstairs. He mumbled something to me about the poor singing.

"Well, you should have been up here playing the guitar," I said.

He didn't answer and went back downstairs. I went to my room to get ready for bed. Kneeling beside the bed, I prayed for Tim. God spoke to me and I knew that Tim was going to be afraid downstairs and would come up and ask us to pray for him. I got into bed and a few moments later there was a knock on the door.

Alfred opened the door and there stood Tim, as white as a sheet. "You won't believe what happened. I was downstairs reading a story about a boy in India. He thought that he was following God and then found out that he was deceived and following Satan. Please pray for me. I don't want to be deceived and follow Satan."

Tim came into our room and sat on a chair beside our bed and we laid hands on him and prayed. We rebuked Satan and pled the blood of Jesus. After awhile we asked Tim how he felt.

"Better," he said, but he was still trembling from his waist down. We continued to pray until he felt peace all over.

He said, "I know that I will never renounce God and be deceived by Satan."

Tim left home with our blessing and a promise that he would stay in a Christian commune. Yet when he moved to Vancouver, the influences he encountered weren't all positive. Slowly he began drifting away from God. He would come home and tell us some of the things he was doing, perhaps wanting to shock us and see how we would react. We kept praying for him.

Alfred decided that he should go on a 40-day fast. At the time he had a big project laying blocks. He was unable to take time off work so he fasted and continued to lay blocks. He was only drinking liquids and lost a lot of weight, but he continued his fast for all 40 days. The night before he broke his fast he dreamt that a friend offered him a Kentucky Fried turkey drumstick. I guess we'll never know what the fast accomplished, but he did

Alfred on his 40 day fast

what he felt God was leading him to do. Obeying God was very important to him and God honours obedience.

From Campbell River we moved to Victoria, BC where Alfred and I worked at The Cridge Center as counsellors for couples. Later Alfred became an assistant pastor at Trinity Christian Centre. We started having open house after church on Sundays at our Halliburton farm. Our youth, university students and people from other churches would come by to eat. After lunch, the adults would fellowship and the youth would play sports and hang out together.

It was a very special time for people. We all went back to church in the evening. Some of our children even met their spouses through fellowshipping at the farm.

Eunice remained at home the longest. She really enjoyed being home and was not in a hurry to leave. Eunice attended the University of Victoria and studied hard for her English degree while eating tons of raisins.

I got a job working at the hospital and with all of the kids gone except Mark and Eunice, I was able to save some money. Eunice and I were able to take several trips together. We went to Hawaii for a one-week holiday, which was wonderful. We really enjoyed spending time together.

After Eunice graduated from university we took a trip to Yellowstone Park and then went on to Moosehorn to visit my family. It was April so we didn't expect snow, but it was coming down thickly. The Yellowstone Lodge was the only accommodation around but it was full so I went into the lobby and lay down on a couch by the fire. Eunice didn't want to sleep inside because we hadn't paid to stay, so she went to sleep in the car. At four or five in the morning Eunice came in because she was so cold. We played Scrabble together until the morning. There was so much snow that there was no way out except an old back road along the Oregon Trail. It was narrow and bumpy but we made it safely through to Montana, then across the border to Canada.

Chapter 12
A Hard Goodbye

In 1986, Eunice had just given birth to twins in Victoria, so I went down to help her. While there, I heard that Youth With A Mission (YWAM) had a ship called the *Anastasis*, which had been in Victoria and was now in San Diego. They were asking for volunteers to go and help with a building project in Mexico after a major earthquake there. Alfred and I decided to join the *Anastasis* in San Diego. Alfred worked doing carpentry onboard while I worked in housekeeping.

The Anastasis

The *Anastasis* was like a floating hotel, with about 350 people on board including the crew and volunteers. The first day out of San Diego, I tripped on an electrical cord and broke my arm. It couldn't be x-rayed while we were sailing so I had to wait to have it treated until I got to Mexico. When we arrived in Mexico the chief of police, the mayor and other dignitaries welcomed us. Everyone was looking forward to the "Mercy Ship." We had brought a fire engine, an ambulance, tons of clothing and building material to be distributed to the earthquake survivors.

After some time, Alfred began having physical problems that the ship doctors couldn't diagnose. They recommended that he have more tests done when we returned to Canada. Alfred continued to help with the renovations on the ship, but occasionally he had to take a break. When we returned home to Vancouver he immediately went for more tests.

They performed a colonoscopy and discovered a tumour as large as a baseball in his bowel. Alfred went for immediate surgery. The doctors told us it had been successful and there was no need for further treatment. Alfred recuperated from the surgery and a year later we joined the YWAM School called "Crossroads." We were to take three months of lectures, then we planned to go to Africa and fulfil Alfred's long-ago dream. During our studies at the school, Alfred came down with a high fever. The doctors couldn't figure out why. After many tests, they discovered that the bowel cancer had now spread to his liver. The doctor told us he had about three months to live. We prayed fervently for God to heal him. One night when he was in severe pain, he cried out to God, "Heal me or take me to heaven!"

The pain left and he had great peace. In the morning he got up, dressed, went shopping and mowed the lawn. He knew that God had healed him. Several days later he went to see his doctor, who sent him for more tests to confirm the healing. The tests came back with no sign of cancer. The doctors couldn't believe the tests and argued, accusing one another of having made the wrong diagnosis. We knew that God had healed him and didn't pay attention to what the doctors said.

Sometime later they did more tests, which showed an increase in cancer cells. He went to the cancer clinic for more tests and the doctors found a growth in the liver. It was in a different location than the first time and was a primary cancer, not spread from the bowel as the first had been. We were upset and confused, wondering why God would heal one cancer and allow another one to grow. The doctor told us this was a fast-growing cancer and Alfred would not have much time. We told God that since He'd healed the slow-growing cancer, He'd have no problem healing the fast-growing cancer. We prayed with confidence, trusting God for a miracle. Yet, the more we prayed, the weaker Alfred became. I and several of the students at Crossroads School began to fast and pray.

On the ninth day of my fast Fern came to visit and asked, "Mom, how long are you going to fast?"

"Well, I read the story about Paul fasting in a storm on the way to Rome. After he fasted ten days, God told him to eat and everyone on the ship would be saved. I'll stop on the tenth day – tomorrow."

The next morning I planned to eat and go to class. I was in the bathtub when the phone rang. As I hurried out of the tub to answer the phone I slipped and fell on the floor, passing out. Although he was weak Alfred dragged me to the bedside and called Grace, who lived upstairs. She drove me to emergency.

While I waited for an X-ray the nurse asked, "When was the last time you had something to eat?"

"Ten days ago."

She laughed, thinking I was joking.

"No, really," I said. "My husband has cancer and I'm fasting and praying for God to work a miracle."

"I'm glad to meet you," she said. "I've never met anyone who fasted for ten days."

Just then, the head nurse came up to us and asked me, "Are you Edna Adam?"

"Yes."

"Your husband has just been brought into emergency by ambulance."

When my X-rays came back, they showed that I'd broken my arm badly and would have to stay in the hospital for several days. In the hospital, Alfred was downstairs with a high fever and I was upstairs with a broken arm. I called Crossroads and told them what had happened. They couldn't believe what they heard - why did things get worse after they fasted and prayed? I had no good answers to give them.

Where was God? Why wasn't He answering our prayers? Some of the students came to visit and to encourage us. They sang, "I am a wounded soldier for the Lord. I am not discouraged." I felt encouraged and knew that God had heard our prayers. All things would work out for good. After a few days in the hospital I went home, but Alfred stayed.

He was still getting worse and the doctors said there was nothing they could do for him. He was sent home to die. We continued to pray, asking God for a miracle. Many people stopped by to encourage Alfred, but came away being encouraged by him instead. As Alfred grew weaker and weaker, all the family gathered to be with us. Although Alfred was on morphine, some of the things he said seemed prophetic and we'd write them down. One night everyone had been up late and everyone except Grace and I went out for a walk. As Grace and I sat with Alfred, he took his last breath.

"It's over," I said.

We sat looking at him, thinking our own thoughts. When the others arrived back from their walk, they felt bad that they hadn't been there when he died.

Tim began singing a hymn, then said, "Don't call the undertaker yet. Let's have our own wake tonight."

So we all sat up together that night and talked about funeral arrangements. At the funeral, many of Alfred's friends came and shared what his life had meant to them, those who had known him the longest sharing first.

Shortly before Alfred died, Daniel asked him how he wanted to be remembered, filming his response.

Alfred said, "I think I would like to be remembered as someone who was inwardly deeply attached to his entire family as well as to his spouse. I would like to be remembered most of all by my family and friends as one who really loved God, who really was honest with God and who in his heart probably had a greater commitment and sacrificial standing before God than was seen outwardly."

I think this is exactly how he has been remembered and I knew that Alfred had been welcomed into Heaven and would be there waiting for us.

After Alfred's funeral I spent some time in Yellowknife with Daniel and his wife Kathie and my grandchildren Joshua and Jesika. It was a very healing time for me. I spent a lot of time reading and recovering from the loss of Alfred.

I was reflecting on the funeral and wondering what I should do now that I was single again. When Kathie gave me a book to read I came across this poem:

Crossroads

*When you stand at life's crossroads and view what you think is the
    end*

God has a much bigger vision and He tells you it's only a bend

The road goes on and is smoother and the pause in the song is a rest

*And the part that's unsung and unfinished is the sweetest and richest
    and best*

*So you can rest and relax and grow stronger; let go and let God share
    your load*

*Your work is not finished or ended; you've just come to a bend in the
    road*

I read and re-read those words and found comfort. I knew that I had come to a bend in the road, but my life was not over - God had more for me to do.

Chapter 13
Too Old for What?

After finishing the lecture phase at Crossroads, I applied to go on the *Anastasis*, which was now stationed in Africa. I deeply wanted to go to Africa and fulfill Alfred's vision, but I received a reply back from the ship saying that I was too old. This answer was very disappointing as I was only sixty-four and in good health. I asked them to please reconsider my request, but received the same answer - too old. Still, I knew that God had more for me to do, so I asked the question, "Too old for what?"

Instead of going to Africa, I moved from Vancouver to Kelowna, BC and joined the staff of the Crossroads school in Winfield. Crossroads is for people who are retired or have lost a loved one. The subjects are carefully chosen to encourage and give purpose to the students.

When I was a student, the class that was most helpful to me was called "The Plumb Line." This class taught us how to make adjustments and line up with God's purpose for our lives. In some ways it was similar to a twelve-step program. I learned about my weaknesses and strengths and that understanding what I'd inherited from my parents was important. From my parents, I received my raw material. They gave me a blueprint for my future, negative and positive, handicapped and healthy. I learned that life isn't always fair, but it's important to face reality.

Crossroads also taught me that God is a God of redemption. He can redeem the raw material and weave it into a beautiful pattern for His glory and my good. I can then choose to own my story, both the painful chapters and the happy ones. One of my many lifelong struggles has been rejection. All through life I've felt like the fifth wheel on a wagon or the spare tire on a car. "The Plumb Line" taught me that God doesn't make junk. I'm special and have value, because I am made in His image.

During my years at Crossroads, I had the opportunity to take many trips to travel and do outreach. At age 65 I went to Hawaii to YWAM's University of the Nations to take a course in video production. I was interested in taking videos of my family and thought this course would help. On my flight to Hawaii, I prayed that God would send someone special to sit beside me, but the seat beside me remained empty. We were about to take off when a younger lady took the seat beside me – the last one available. She said, "I don't know why I'm on this plane or in this seat."

"I do," I said.

"What do you mean?"

"I've been praying that God would bring someone special to sit with me."

"Well, I guess I'm that special person. Why did you pray that prayer?"

I told her why I was going to Hawaii and began to share about my family and my faith in God. She told me she and her friends had been skiing in Whistler. That morning, she'd suddenly felt the urge to leave her friends and take a plane back to Australia via Hawaii. She'd arrived late at the airport and almost missed her flight. She told me she'd recently decided to go back to church after many years of not attending, but couldn't find a church where she felt comfortable. We talked the whole way to Hawaii. As we said goodbye, I handed her a book called "Inside Out," written by Larry Crab, a psychologist. She was also a psychologist so she was interested and promised to read it.

"Keep it and pass it onto others," I said.

In Hawaii, I discovered that I'd signed up for a one year university course condensed into three months. Often I felt frustrated because I had to learn so many professional lighting and sound techniques that I had no intention of using, but I kept persevering. I enjoyed being with the young people in the school and I ended up getting the highest marks in my class.

At age 66 I took a team of seniors to Russia. We were there for nine weeks with other groups from different countries and numbered about 150 in total. Russia respects grey hair. I spoke at high schools and when I told them that I had seven children and twenty-two grandchildren, the students would sit up and listen. Then I would share my testimony, telling them that God loves them and has a plan for their lives. Many were eager to receive Jesus as their saviour.

One of our Russian guides warned us to look out for the mafia because they were watching us. He had been in the mafia for 15 years, so he knew how to spot them. Eddie, a Samoan with the

Hong Kong dance team, was invited to visit a Russian friend in his home. While he was there visiting, the mafia arrived, threatening Eddie's Russian friend. They wanted to take him out to the park and shoot him. Eddie got between the mafia and his friend and said, "Leave him alone – take me."

"Okay, come outside."

They led him downstairs and out to their car. "Get in the car and we'll take you to the park and shoot you."

"Why would you take me to the park?" Eddie asked. "Why not just shoot me here?"

"Oh, okay, never mind," they said and left.

When Eddie shared this story with us the next day, our guide said, "Never go to Russian homes, never go outside at night and be very careful. Keep your eyes open."

One day a group of us were in the market and I was filming the scene. A member of the mafia came up and put his hand over my camera lens. "Don't take any pictures!"

I thought he would take my camera, but he left me and I hastily put my camera away. That reinforced the warnings and from then on I left my camera at home.

At age 67 I took a team to the Ukraine where my parents were born. We traveled by local transportation, visiting schools, universities, prisons and hospitals and had many adventures.

One day I was on my way home by bus after dark. My roommate had missed the bus so I was on my own. When I got off at the bus stop and began walking to the house where we were staying, I realized I was lost and had no idea where I was. I didn't know the street name or house number of the place I was staying. I couldn't speak any Ukrainian and nobody spoke English. The skies were cloudy and rain was imminent. Scared and wondering what to do, I prayed and asked God for guidance. Then I remembered to look in my fanny pack, where I found our hostess' phone number. I hurried to a pay phone and called for help. Her daughter answered the phone and I told her, "I got off at a bus stop but I'm not sure if it's the right one."

"I'll be right there to get you," she said.

As I waited in the dark, it began to rain. Soon it was pouring and I was not only scared but soaking wet and cold. My friend was nowhere in sight. I called again and discovered that the daughter couldn't find me and had returned home worried, wondering where I could be. I described some of the buildings around me to her and she told me that I had got off the bus two stops too soon. She soon arrived to rescue me. I was very happy and apologized for all the trouble I had caused. I also thanked God for helping me find the phone number. What I would have done without it? How frightening it is to be lost in a strange country when you don't speak the language.

We spent nine weeks in the Ukraine and had a wonderful time sharing God's love, seeing many souls come to Jesus.

In the spring of that year, I began to feel discouraged. This was just after the Oklahoma City Bombing and I was concerned over world events as well as things happening in my own family. As I sat praying, I fell asleep and heard a voice saying, "Awaken!" Wondering what this meant, I sat down to write a letter to God.

April 10, 1991

Dear God,

It is I, Your servant Edna. I feel rotten and need to talk to You, so I am writing you a letter. Please read it and get back to me as soon as possible. I really need Your help, God. I feel lousy and trapped, restless and tired. I find it hard to pray and read Your Word. Oh yes, I have a burden to pray and I do pray. But I feel overwhelmed, wondering what is happening in this world. Is the end near? You say in 2 Peter 3:9 that You are not willing that any should perish. I know that You are a loving God and I believe that You are in control, but it sure would be encouraging to know what You are up to and how I can be of help down here, where the rubber meets the road. But by faith I choose to trust You, because there is no one else here on Earth or in Heaven. The Hindu idols have ears but can't hear; they have eyes but can't see. Buddha is dead. Nirvana is nothingness.

So God; I guess you are stuck with me. I will trust and follow You until the end of my life. Your faithfulness to me right now is and over the past years has been, awesome.

I continued on, writing about my concerns for my family and for world events. Concluding, I wrote,

I need Your help so please speak to me with a few more words and make them simple, because I don't have much education. But You say in Your Word that You choose the foolish of this world to shame the wise, the weak to shame the strong and the things that are not to nullify the things that are, so that no one may boast before You. Thank You that You give hope and encouragement to the broken and hurting people. Thank You for giving me hope.

P.S. Sorry God for this long letter, but I feel much better. Please teach me how to pray more effectively for my family.

After the word "awaken," I felt convicted about spending too much time watching TV. I decided to buy a large picture of Jesus, which I put in front of the TV. Every time I wanted to watch TV, I had to ask Jesus' permission to do so. One time Alfred's brother Herald came over with his wife to visit me and asked, "Where's your TV?"

"It's there behind the picture of Jesus. If you want to watch TV, you'll have to move Jesus out of the way."

When I was 68, I went with a group to Taiwan and Hong Kong. I loved filming my trips but everyone told me not to film so much. One day I saw a Taiwanese funeral going on and decided to get some footage.

"Edna, you can't film a funeral!" my team members scolded me, but afterwards they were glad that I had documented all our adventures.

At age 69 I was on staff at Crossroads in Hawaii, where I helped facilitate and run small groups.

After Hawaii, I took a team from Kelowna to India and Nepal, where I had the opportunity to visit people from my past in India and even to meet with and pray for Mother Theresa in Calcutta. I met with Dinah Mary and found that she had never married but had remained a nurse and a strong Christian. Although Rajani had passed away from cancer when her children were quite young, I was able to meet all her children, who were dedicated Christians. One of her daughters was working with Wycliffe and had translated the Bible into Bhutanese, while her son-in-law was a lab technician in Bhutan.

Howard shared his memories of our trip to India with me.

My trip to India was most memorable mostly because of who I went with, a seasoned missionary named Edna. She knew the Indian culture and language for the most part. When the seven of us landed in the Calcutta airport we picked up our luggage and headed outside to catch a taxi. That's when all chaos broke loose. Who was going to be our taxi driver? An argument ensued as our luggage was grabbed from us and headed in three directions. Then Edna yelled out some words she remembered from the language. Within minutes our luggage returned. Edna negotiated the cab fares quickly and off into the night we went. After about an hour the driver was still trying to find the address we had given him. Once in awhile the driver would stop and ask for directions. Another hour went by - still no results on the address. We were getting little concerned. Most of us were in culture shock; after all this was Calcutta and the poverty we witnessed was shocking.

Then came a breakthrough - the driver had found the YWAM base. We turned into a large driveway and the gates opened. They closed behind us and we drove down the well-lit driveway. We pulled up in front of a large building that looked like a king's palace. Well, I thought, at last Edna has delivered! Now we wouldn't have to stay outside those gates.

The uniformed bellboys came out to take our luggage and as we followed them inside Edna said, "Well, YWAM went all out on this one! Imagine staying in a palace with marble floors, servants, and who knows what else."

Within minutes, reality set in. This was not the YWAM base but a country club for the rich in Calcutta.

We were disappointed, but Edna cleared things up by saying, "I thought this was too nice of a place to be YWAM."

Off we went in our taxis again and eventually we did find the YWAM base. This was our first five hours in India with Edna. Two days later we took a train across the plains of West Bengal and up to Siliguri. We tried to get first class seats but to no avail. We settled for second class and Edna just said, "Well, everyone else rides second class."

From Siliguri we took an old Jeep up into the Himalayan Mountains. The road was narrow and steep, and as we got up higher into the mountains I thought for sure we would go over the edge.

Edna could read my face and said, "What's the matter, Howard?

Are you afraid?" in a way that only she could say.

I shot up a prayer then lied and said, "No, not at all." We did make it safely up to Darjeeling. The thing that touched me the most was when Edna was reunited with several local ladies that had come to know the Lord through her and Al's ministry there thirty years earlier. These ladies would sit at the edge of Edna's bed until she went to sleep then return before she woke in the morning. What a testimony. I could see the fruit of Edna and Al's work everywhere we went in India.

One other thing Edna did was got us in to have a private little meeting with Mother Theresa. It happened that the day before our visit Mother Theresa had gotten a dog bite on her arm so Edna prayed over her. Throughout the trip I admired Edna's strength, determination and her faith to go and do all she did, knowing God was with her.

After my visit to India I went to spend the summer in Yellowknife helping Kathie run her bed and breakfast. While there I heard about a tour to Israel and asked Kathie if she wanted to go with me. Kathie decided to go and paid me to work at the B&B to help me pay my way. We went with a church group from Ottawa and Kelowna and saw many famous places from the Bible.

Me and Kathie in Jerusalem

We also went to see the holocaust museum and some of the Jewish communes that had been threatened by the war.

The conflict in the area was evident, with discarded tanks on both sides of the road. One day while we were returning to our hotel, the police stopped all traffic because there was an oncoming bus with a suspicious package. I filmed the police as they took the package out of the bus and opened it. After blowing it up, they discovered it wasn't a bomb and we were allowed to continue to our hotel.

After Israel we went to Greece to visit places from the Apostle Paul's travels. We took a cruise to different islands, one of which no cars were allowed and was very peaceful. Just outside of Athens we went to Mars Hill where Paul had preached his famous sermon about the "unknown god." Everything looked exactly how I would have imagined it to be in Paul's day.

Just before I turned 70 I was finally able to go to Africa. I went to Muizenberg, South Africa for three months to attend YWAM's School of Intercession and Spiritual Warfare. The day before I left I went to the bank to get some money for my trip. On my way home I was driving slowly, looking for a second-hand store to do last-minute shopping. Suddenly, a big, muscular man opened the door of my car on the driver's side and sat down on top of me. "Go quickly!" he yelled.

I tried to unbuckle my seatbelt so I could get out from under him. My car was a standard and had stalled. The intruder tried to start it but before he could do so, hands reached through the half-open door and pulled him out of the car. A policeman wrestled him to the ground and handcuffed him. At the same time several more police cars arrived on the scene. It all happened so fast that I sat in my car stunned, feeling like I was watching a movie.

The sheriff came to speak to me. "Are you alright ma'am?" he asked. "Do you know that man?"

"I've never seen him before," I said.

At first they didn't believe me, because they thought that I was the getaway car. I was told that this man was in the courthouse being charged for a crime he had committed in Victoria. After the charges he bolted, jumped through the window and ran across the parking lot and into my car, which was going very slowly.

Eventually I convinced them I wasn't the getaway car. The sheriff apologized and asked if he could drive me home. I assured him that I was able to drive home on my own. That evening he came to visit me and I told him that I was on my way to South Africa in the morning. He told me that he was a Christian and on his way to a prayer meeting.

The next morning I bought a local newspaper. On the front page was a picture of my car with the caption, "Prisoner's escape bid cut short." Suddenly I realized the seriousness of what had happened. What if the convict had gotten away in my car with me as a hostage? The police would have chased us and perhaps caused an accident and I could have been killed. Or if he'd got away with me as his hostage, who knows what might have happened? God protected me from harm and I had a great story to tell to my grandchildren.

My White Toyota

The YWAM base in Muizenberg was in a hotel called "Surfer's Paradise" and was right on the beach. There were colourful shacks in red, yellow, blue and green in a row along the white sand, which stretched for miles. You could walk along the beach in the morning and find all kinds of beautiful seashells. It would sometimes get very windy and blow so much sand onto the road that they would have to clear it with sand ploughs.

In the school we learned different techniques for praying against the powers of darkness. One day I had to give a talk on intercession. While I was praying about what I should share, I got a picture of a chess board. I'd never played chess and I didn't know what it meant, so I went to the library to get a book on the history of chess. It said that there are two sides to the game, usually symbolized by black and white pieces. The game is one of warfare in which you actively engage with the enemy. I realized this was a metaphor for spiritual warfare.

While I was planning my talk one Saturday afternoon, there was a knock on my door. I opened the door to find a young man and a young woman who were Jehovah's Witnesses. I invited them in. I had been drawing a chess board and they asked me why. They played chess and they were very intrigued to hear about how chess symbolized spiritual warfare. The next Saturday they came back again and wanted to hear more about what I was going to teach on. This was a confirmation to me about the importance of the message. I decided to share about how the book of Esther was like a game of chess between the powers of good and evil. I made myself a sackcloth smock to wear and the students were quite intrigued by my presentation.

I spent my 70th birthday in Muizenberg. All the young men honoured me, sending flowers and inviting me to a German festival, escorting me there and back. As the oldest woman there, I got the special treatment.

One day I was walking on the beach when I saw a well-dressed, grey-haired lady sitting on a bench staring out at the sea. She looked lonely so I sat down beside her, asking, "May I join you?"

"Yes," she said. She seemed tired and I could see sadness in her eyes. "Where are you from?"

"Canada."

"Canada. My sister was married to a Canadian. He was a wonderful man. What are you doing in South Africa?"

"Well, I'm attending a school called 'Intercessory Prayer and Spiritual Warfare.'"

"Really? I've never heard of it."

I began sharing stories about my experiences at the school. She listened attentively and I wanted to keep sharing, but it was time for me to go back to class.

"Can I take you to lunch one day?" she asked.

"Well, I'll have to get permission from my teacher, but I'll let you know the answer."

When I got permission the next day, I called the woman, whose name was Doris. Doris picked up her sister and me and we went to the golf club restaurant. They both belonged to the golf club. On the way, I shared my story, telling them about my childhood and how Jesus had changed my life. They were very attentive and asked,

"Will you come and share at our ladies' club?"

The ladies' club met once a month for lunch and since it was almost Christmas, they asked if I could come and share at the Christmas luncheon. Doris' sister was the president so she arranged for speakers. Although exams were just before Christmas, I got permission to speak at the club. "What should I wear?" I asked, "Formal, or informal?"

"Informal," Doris told me.

"What does that mean in your club?" I asked.

"Oh, just a silk blouse and a skirt."

My version of informal was much more casual and I didn't have either a silk blouse or a skirt with me, but I managed to borrow both. I shared more of my story with the women at the club and invited them to tour the YWAM medical ship that was arriving in port in a few weeks. I gave Doris a book called, "Is that Really You, God?" by Lorne Cunningham, YWAM's founder. Afterwards the women told me how much they enjoyed my talk and came to tour the ship when it arrived.

On my way back from South Africa I prayed for someone interesting to sit beside me. With an empty seat beside me I travelled to Korea, where I had to switch planes. A Fijian woman got on the plane and sat beside me and we began to talk. She lived in Edmonton but taught school in Korea and was on her way home for Christmas. She told me that she was a Muslim.

"Tell me about Islam," I said.

She shared a bit but said, "I'm not a good Muslim."

"What do they teach about sin and the forgiveness of sin?" I asked.

"That's one thing I don't like about Islam," she said. "They don't have any answers to the sin question. Not like you Christians; you teach that Jesus died for your sins and that you can be forgiven."

I was surprised and asked, "How do you know so much about Christianity?"

"My friend in Edmonton took me to church."

"Why aren't you a Christian?"

"Well, my parents are Muslim and I was born a Muslim."

I shared my testimony with her, telling her what the Bible teaches about Jesus, God and sin. For the next twelve hours we studied the Scriptures. She was extremely interested and gave me her address. I promised to send her a book called "The Torn Veil," the story of a Muslim girl whom Jesus appeared to and healed from a severe illness after which she became a Christian and suffered terrible persecution from her family. She gladly promised to read it. When I arrived home I sent the book to her. She wrote back saying she really enjoyed the book but was not ready to become a

Christian because of her lifestyle. She said she definitely was not a good Muslim but needed more time to think about Christianity. Encouraging her to continue to be open and learn about God and Christianity, I told her to ask Jesus to reveal Himself to her. I never heard back from her but continued to pray for her.

The Hells Angels Motorcycle Club is infamous worldwide but Canada has more members per capita than any other country. One summer a group of Hells Angels from Eastern Canada came for a convention in Kelowna. Knowing their reputation, I began praying for them. While praying, I felt an urge to go to the hotel where they were staying and invite them to come to my church on Sunday. This impression seemed so strange that I struggled with whether it was really from God. When I shared it with my prayer group they encouraged me to obey and see what would happen. I invited a man from my church along with me and he said he'd go the next morning.

However, by the evening I felt such a restless urgency I decided to go down to the hotel myself. I waited until 9 pm then very slowly walked downtown to the hotel. There were Harley motorcycles parked all over the sidewalk in front of the hotel and cops pacing back and forth. Feeling nervous, I kept walking. When I reached the hotel entrance, in the doorway stood a biker so tall he looked like Goliath. I felt as small as David but I didn't even have a sling.

I looked up at him and said, "Hello, my name is Granny Adam and I'd like to welcome you to Kelowna."

He looked down and put out his hand. "Well thanks Granny, my name's Greg."

We shook hands and I asked him, "Tell me about the Hells Angels. Which do you relate more to - the Hell or the Angels?"

"The Angels I guess," he replied.

"Do you have a grandmother?"

"Yes I do."

"Is she a praying grandmother?"

"Yes. I believe she's praying for me."

"Well if your grandmother's praying for you, you don't have a chance. God will answer her prayer."

The girls in the hotel kept calling him, but he wanted to talk with me. I invited him to church and told him to bring all his friends. I could imagine them arriving at church and revving their bikes as people at the church began freaking out. Greg said, "Granny Adam, thank you. I promise if we're still in town on Sunday we'll be there. But we're planning to leave for Vancouver on Saturday." I left for home, and it wasn't 'til later that I realized I'd been so excited that I'd forgot to tell him the time of the service. I went back to the hotel on Saturday morning to tell him but they were gone. If I'd gone on Saturday as I'd originally planned, I never would have met Greg.

It was shortly after this that I went to South Africa. After three months I came back and was asked to share at a church in Victoria. I felt led to share about the divine appointment I'd had with the Hell's Angels. At the end of the service the pastor gave an invitation for anyone that had a need to come forward for prayer. Up the aisles came a tall, good-looking man. He looked at me and said, "Sock it to me, Granny Adam."

After I prayed for him he told me he knew Greg and had ridden with the Hells Angels. He started crying as he told me how his wife had left him and his 13-year old daughter was going astray. Because of this he had left the Hells Angels. This was the first time he'd ever been to church and a friend had invited him to the service.

I and others gathered around him and prayed for him to receive Jesus. Although I never found out what happened to Greg, I knew that God had brought this man to Him through my story.

Often I would go for walks in the park in Kelowna. Sometimes I'd be in a hurry and wouldn't stop to talk to people. Other times I'd see groups of young people sitting around playing their guitars and singing and I'd sit with them.

"I'm Granny Adam," I'd say. "Do you have grandparents?" Some hated their parents, but they sure loved to talk about their grandparents. I would ask them if their grandparents prayed for them. They would usually answer, "Yes, my grandmother prays for me." Then I would tell them, "I have twenty-two wonderful grandchildren that I pray for every day. I'd tell them how important it was to make right choices in favour of God and that God had a plan for their lives. They would listen and ask questions and I found it easy to talk to them.

Several times I was asked to share at young peoples' gatherings held at my church. Three to four thousand young people would gather from all over B.C. and Washington. I would sit in an old rocking chair wearing granny clothes and a wig and share stories about my life when I was their age. I told them about God's faithfulness and then asked them to imagine themselves my age. Would they be satisfied with how they had lived their lives, or would they have regrets? I challenged them to make right choices while they were still young. After the service they gathered around me asking questions. Some would say, "I don't have grandparents - will you be my grandmother?"

I felt no generation gap; young people want to hear what grandparents have to say about God's faithfulness.

One day I was walking to the grocery store in Kelowna. I saw a lady at the bus stop holding a young child and wearing a very colourful dress. Curious about the dress, I stopped and asked her where she was from.

"Somalia," she said.

"Really? What are you doing in Kelowna?"

"I'm a refugee and I'm studying English."

"Would you like to come to church with me on Sunday?""Well, I'm a Muslim...""We welcome Muslims. You also believe in the God of Abraham, Isaac and Jacob."The woman, whose name was Saida, came to the church service and after it was finished, began

telling me her story: "One day I went to the market to shop. While I was there, the shooting began. I started to run following the crowd, and then I finally arrived in Nairobi where I stayed in a refugee camp. Most of my family didn't make it out of Somalia. Only my mother and one brother made it to the refugee camp. At the camp I worked at the hospital. One day a newborn baby was brought to the hospital and we looked for the mother, but couldn't find her. They asked me to look after the baby."

This was the young child she had with her; because she had adopted her she was able to come to Canada. The young girl loved Sunday school and Saida kept coming to church until she moved to Surrey, BC. Before she left she asked me to help her find a church in Surrey, so I connected her with my friends there and they took her to church. I kept in touch with her for a long time and still pray for her and her family.

One day while I was waiting for my prescription at Safeway I met Emily. She complained about her aches and pains. I asked, "Can I be of any help?"

"I need a new body," she mumbled.

"Do you know about the Great Physician, who works miracles?" I asked her.

I asked her if she knew what happens after death. She said no. I started sharing scriptures about death and Heaven with her. Then she was called for her prescription. She quickly gave me her phone number and asked me to call her. I gave her a call and she invited me over to her house for tea. She was lonely and needed someone to talk to. She told me about finding her daughter, whom she had given up for adoption 64 years ago. Sharing with her about Jesus, I told her what a wonderful place He's preparing for us in Heaven, where there won't be any more pain or tears.

"How can I be sure if I'm going to Heaven when I die?" she asked.

I prayed with her and she received Jesus into her life. I continued to visit her until I left Kelowna.

Chapter 14
Romance at the Fountain of Youth

It had been forty years since I'd had the vision in Kurseong of the angel and the map of the "land of roses." At age 72, I finally fulfilled that dream. I arrived for the winter at the Fountain of Youth (FOY) near the Salton Sea in Southern California. There, life begins at 70. I was staying with my friend Jean but I wanted a place of my own. One day I went for a walk and saw a small trailer for sale. The price was right, but I had no money to buy it. I called my son Daniel and told him about the trailer. He was excited and asked how much money I needed to buy the trailer.

When I told him he said, "No problem, we wanted to give you some money for Christmas."

I bought the trailer and moved in, sure that God had a plan for

me at the FOY. One day my friend Lois introduced me to Joe Simpson. My first impression was that he was tall, handsome and good-looking. I had been a widow for about thirteen years and wasn't looking for a husband. I was looking for someone to help me with the rock wall I was working on. What I really needed was a truck to haul some rocks! The first words out of my mouth were, "Do you have a truck?"

Joe did have a truck and he hauled rocks for me that Saturday. On Sunday he showed up at church and asked if he could sit with me. After the service I invited him to my place for lunch to repay him for hauling the rocks. After lunch he went back to Slab City, a rudimentary trailer park built on the slabs from the old army encampment. He was camped there with a group of singles and I didn't see him again that year.

The next winter I was busy painting the inside of my trailer when I heard a knock on the door. I opened the door and there was Joe. I was very excited to see him and gave him a big hug. At first, I hadn't been interested in him, but now I felt a sudden rush of emotion. After Alfred had died I'd been numb as far as romantic feelings were concerned, so I was surprised by the intensity of my emotion.

After we had lunch together, Joe went back to the Slabs, but the next day he showed up at bocce ball and watched while I played. After the game he invited me to have lunch with him at the restaurant. I really liked his company and we became friends.

I had another project that I needed help with. A friend of mine had given me an add-on or "California room." I needed a truck to haul it to my place and a handyman to help me attach it to my trailer. Joe offered to haul it to my place but wasn't sure about helping with the rest of the project because he was on his way to hike in the Big Bend Park in Texas. I had to beg him to stay and help me. It was a big project but we had fun working together. He was impressed by how much I knew about using power tools and building. I told him I'd learned a lot from building houses with Alfred. Joe stayed until the project was nearly completed, when I could handle the rest by myself.

He left for Texas and a week later I received a letter from someone named "Verley." I discovered this was Joe's first name. We corresponded and decided to attend the Calgary Stampede together in July and visit Daniel and his family in Yellowknife. Joe arrived in Victoria and we visited with my family and then we took a trip across Vancouver Island. We travelled to the Calgary Stampede where I'd made arrangements to stay with friends at the YWAM base near Calgary.

On our way we stopped in Edmonton to visit my friends Jack and Winnie. After a few days in Edmonton with Winnie and Jack, we travelled on to Yellowknife to visit Daniel and Kathie. It was summertime so the sun hardly set and Joe and I went for long walks by Great Slave Lake.

Daniel asked, "What are your plans with Joe, Mom?"

"We're just friends," I told him. But I think he knew better.

We returned to Victoria and Joe went back to California. He promised to take the train back to Washington and meet me at his son's place and then help me drive to California. Joe kept his promise and took the long train ride up to Washington. We spent a few days at his son's place, did some sightseeing and then headed to California to meet his daughter and family. I was glad that we could travel together and that Joe did most of the driving. After staying a few days at his daughter's place, I left for the FOY. Joe had plans to go to Death Valley and said he would meet me later at FOY on his way to Slab City. He still hadn't mentioned marriage and by this point I was getting a bit frustrated. Joe arrived at the FOY and we enjoyed swimming in the pool together and playing bocce.

One day when we were in the pool I said, "Joe, I love you and I want to know what your feelings are towards me."

He told me that he was falling in love and asked, "When do you want to get married?

I said, "Yesterday!"

We made wedding plans for January 9, 1999. We got married at

Our Wedding

the FOY. All of Joe's family and most of my family attended. We had a wonderful wedding with many of our friends pitching in to help.

I asked my friend Margaret to sing at our wedding and this is how she remembered it.

I attended the Ladies' Bible Study and met Edna there, where she was the teacher. She told us a bit about her interesting life as a missionary, and she was a good Bible teacher. I never missed a class. At the Fountain of Youth, I had several opportunities to sing special numbers, and after singing a solo one evening for Fun Night program, Edna asked me to sing for her upcoming wedding to Joe Simpson.

I was happy to accept this invitation, and looked forward to learning the song she requested, and singing it for their wedding..

When morning arrived the day of the wedding, a calamity occurred, and I could not sing; in fact, I could not even speak. My voice was silent. I was so very disappointed, and had to inform them that I could not sing as requested. Our good friend John Janzen took my place, and I know he did a fine job for them too. I was sad to miss this wedding, and heard later how very nice it was.

As the years go along, Edna and Joe and I have become good friends. We have spent time e-mailing each other, and on occasion have played games together too. We all happily return to the Fountain of Youth each winter.

I praise God for Joe; he truly is a gift. We enjoy playing games and traveling together. We've gone on several cruises, taken a trip to Hawaii and travelled to many places in the states and Canada. It's been wonderful at my age to have a companion to do things with.

I remember what my friend Winnie had to say to me about the FOY and Joe.

I first met Edna, when we were parked at dry camp at FOY. We became friends quickly. She had just bought a small trailer, I think for a thousand dollars. We chummed together a lot, shared recipes, baking, it was a lot of fun. She was a widow and I thought she would be like that forever. On cool evenings I would come over and she was always cold, sitting under a blanket. She would share her "blankie" with me and we would talk about the Lord and other things. It was fun and every year we would renew our friendship. It was the "same place, same station" experience.

I fondly remember that those were happy times. I don't remember how many years went by, but one day I heard some people say "Edna was interested in romance." I couldn't believe it! She had never said anything to me, and besides, people talk so much. I thought Edna was close to seventy five and wouldn't be thinking about romance. I thought no more about it and plus since she was a former missionary, I figured she had better things to do than chasing after a man! I never saw her with anyone and I was not watching her that close. I didn't want to pry into someone else's business; I had enough of my own. As time went on, she talked about a man called Joe. He was from "the slabs". Well what good could come from "the slabs"? One day she was waiting for him and he didn't come. We left to go back to Edmonton without meeting him.

Edna left to go back home to Canada. In the summer, I had a phone call from her mentioning that they would be travelling by Edmonton and if they could stop by our place overnight. I asked Edna, "they"? She said yes, but they would have to have different beds and different rooms. She didn't say if the other person was male or female, but I figured as much. I said that whoever it was would have to sleep in the motor home, where I fixed up a bed. She came with this man named Joe. She said there was nothing going on, so I believed her. I was watching out of the corner of my eye and they were looking into each other's eyes. So, I didn't know whether she spoke the truth or not. I had to hear a little bit more so we went for a little walk. I said "What is this?" You were peeking in each other's eyes. "Winnie", she said, "This is really something. I get goose bumps all over me when he is coming. But really I don't know, there is nothing." I thought that this is hard to believe. I felt she was playing with fire. They stayed a couple of days with Joe sleeping in the motor home and Edna in the spare bedroom. When we went for a walk, I watched them hold hands, but maybe this was because Edna was afraid of falling.

I was anxious and interested to see her the following winter at the FOY. When I saw her I asked her how Joe was doing and if anything was happening. Were they thinking of marriage? She mentioned that Joe hadn't asked her yet and so things continued. One Sunday, Joe asked if they could come over for dinner. We said sure, but it was kind of strange. After dinner, Joe announced that he had something to say. "Edna and I have decided to split up." I didn't believe it at this time because Edna looked so happy. I told him so, and then he said that actually they had decided to get married. This was the first of Joe's jokes, with many more to come. He also said that they had decided not to have any kids...well, that was a relief!

In January, what a wedding it was with their children and friends! Joe and Edna have been happy ever since!

Our travels together have often involved adventures, even in the most ordinary of places. One time when Joe and I were traveling we stopped at McDonalds for lunch. After lunch Joe went to our fifth wheel while I used the bathroom. When I went downstairs to join Joe, I saw him and the fifth wheel across the freeway. How in the world did I end up on the other side of the freeway? I went back upstairs and discovered that this McDonalds was built above the freeway so you could enter it from either side.

My friends wonder how I can travel in foreign countries if I get lost in McDonald's.

"That's why I always take a group of people with me," I say.

I may get lost sometimes, but I still love a good challenge as much as I did when I was a tomboy on the farm in Moosehorn.

One of the things Joe and I discussed when we got married is what to do when we pass on. We decided that Joe would be buried next to his former wife who also died of cancer and I would be buried next to Alfred. It will be some reunion in heaven when we all get there.

When I was 77, we got our first computer, a whole new

challenge for me. My son-in law Ray, who teaches computer at a college, volunteered to give me a few lessons. After that I was on my own learning the hard way, by trial and error. I still call him for help every once in a while and my daughter-in law Kathie as well, and sometimes I think life was a lot easier before the computer. But now I wouldn't know how to get along without one.

I also produce a lot of the bocce ball and shuffleboard certificates for the tournaments at the FOY. It amazes me that at my age I can still overcome any obstacles!

Chapter 15
Reunions

I have seven children, twenty-two grandchildren, seven great-grandchildren and many in-laws. The first time we had most of the family together we were living in Sointula, BC. We had an 8 mm video camera and the sound wasn't very reliable, but we captured many wonderful memories. Our dog Princess romped on the grassy hillside with the kids and everyone played tag and hide-and-seek.

Christmas became a special time at the Bain's big, beautiful home. Grace and her husband Grayson were wonderful hosts. Grace would roast a great big turkey and we would help prepare all the trimmings. After dinner we'd gather around the Christmas tree

to sing carols and open presents with Alfred as Santa Claus. After the younger kids were put to bed the rest of us would play games like Rook and Scrabble. When the games ended, some of us would stay up all night and share from our hearts. These times were a special opportunity to understand each other and bond as a family.

With new grandkids being born all the time, there came a time when there were too many of us to gather at the Bain's home. We decided to camp together in the summer time and each year we found a group campsite near a lake, a river, or the ocean. We played games in a field, went for walks and gathered around the campfire at night to play guitar and sing songs.

One year we camped in Osoyoos, BC, in the Pocket Desert. The men took the younger kids for a "rattlesnake hike" and came across two snakes, one of which slithered towards them. They filmed it as it got closer and closer. When they showed the video to the women back at camp, they were upset that the men had let their children get so close to the rattlesnakes. From then on, some moms made sure they always went on the hikes.

We've had reunions all over BC and Washington and even in India where we got to visit Farley and re-live our past together.

My 80th birthday reunion was very important and I have many wonderful lasting memories from it. Daniel and Kathie, who had a lovely Victorian-style bed and breakfast home in the small seaside town of Ladysmith, BC at the time, hosted it.

Family and friends gathered for my special weekend. On Saturday Kathie prepared a wonderful Indian meal, which brought back memories of our time in India. Some people wore Indian clothes and the living room was draped with Indian material. After we'd all eaten, we crowded into the living room filling all the couches and chairs, spreading onto the floor and stairs. Everyone participated in lively singing, playing guitar, bongo drums, the rain-stick and anything else they could find.

The Bain kids prepared a play using puppets and dollar-store figures for the different members of the family. We could hardly stop laughing at "Timostegosaurus," "Rescue Ruth," "Eunihulk," "Cactus…I mean Fern," "Build-a-Bot Daniel," "Scrabble g.r.a.c.e." puppet Mark with his guitar and Joe and me as little penguins. I was the one with a camera taped to my shoulder.

Eunice and Tom's family filmed a re-enactment of my childhood (including when I'd given Mr. Luckow a black eye) with Elizabeth playing me complete with a straw hat and checked shirt. Others sang special songs for me. Jon Snell had the video camera and took lots of video, which we have watched over and over.

Then it was time for people to share. Tim stood up at the front.

I think the best way we can honor anybody is to recognize and pay attention to their essence. So I'd like you to keep that in mind as we honor Mom, to remind yourself of what it is about Mom that makes her who she is, unique as a woman, and what it is that has caused so many people to gather to honor her. It's something pretty remarkable that people should come so far to honor this woman. So I invite you to speak up from where you are or come to the front to share a story or a memory about this woman that we've come here to honor and to recognize and to affirm.

One by one different people spoke up from around the room. Elsie my sister had come all the way from Moosehorn to share my birthday with me and she shared about our trip together to visit Leo a number of years before.

Edna and I went to Toronto to see Leo. We had a real good trip. When the bus stopped to let everyone else out for a smoke, we went walking. We had a good visit with our brother Leo.

I was glad that I had the opportunity to share my testimony with him, because this was the last time I saw him - he passed away not long after our visit. Although I'd lost both my parents and most of my brothers and sisters, I'd been blessed with so many new family members through my children and grandchildren. Almost all of them had come and I was so proud to see them and hear them share.

Tim's son Julian, who is a well-spoken and talented musician, said,

I'd just like to acknowledge the effort you've put into getting to know every one of us. That's a lot of people. I'm sure it's been some work and by 80 I'm sure some things get a little hazy, but you've managed to sustain a pretty good relationship with everyone.

There certainly were a lot of people in my family, but I loved every one of them and was so glad to know them all. Ruth's son Robert is a talented photographer and had made the last family reunion video. He said,

After doing the last reunion video, I sort of got a look from your angle, always looking through the camera and always videotaping. I don't know if we all appreciate it. I mean, the videos aren't exactly high-action all the time and sometimes they're a little long.

Everyone laughed, thinking of the old videos I'd made with lengthy shots of the kids playing and adults eating, some of the shots repeated multiple times. Robert continued,

I do it all on the computer and I just picture you at home pressing play and record over and over. I think it's a pretty cool thing that you took all that time and all that money. I think the fact that they're long just goes to show that you really like looking at your children and your grandchildren and you're really proud of them. So thanks for all those videos. I think you've left lots for us to look back and see. Keep on trucking!

I was glad too that I'd spent all that time on the videos, because, as Robert said, they become precious time capsules of the past.

Daniel's son Joshua was lying on the floor and waved at the camera.

Hi, it's Joshua here. When you lived with us in Yellowknife you helped me start my first business, my entrepreneurial business. I didn't keep picking up cans but I always sought the most unique method to make a little money and still have fun, through my art or music. I really appreciate you sparking that drive in me and to this day inspiring my thoughts that keep me along that same path. So thank you.

It was true – I'd had so many different jobs in my life and found many creative ways to support my family and myself when I needed to. I knew that creativity was alive and well in my children and grandchildren. It wasn't the only thing that I'd passed on, however.

Daniel, who had become a successful architect and travelled all over the world, shared about something that had always been part of my personality, long before he was born. He said,

One of the constants with you, Mother, through all these years as far as I can remember, is a certain kind of boldness, a boldness that's remarkable for a prairie girl with very limited education. You've never been shy about your faith. Whether people agree with it, whether they have the same values, the same beliefs, you are not shy or ashamed. You've held true to that faith decade after decade after decade. You can sit next to a total stranger on a plane, in a bus depot, in a shopping mall, to the embarrassment of your children sometimes, and you are bold about what you have put your faith in: your God. I really do respect that.

Kathie, who had hosted us with such warmth and has been such a wonderful addition to the family, agreed with Daniel saying,

I worry about when a vacuum cleaner salesman comes to the door because I never know what Mom's going to say. Mom told me a story once about a vacuum salesman who phoned saying, 'I have a free gift for you. I'll just book this vacuum demonstration for you and it's yours.' Then Mom said, 'Wait, wait just a minute - I have a free gift for you,' and she proceeded to tell him about Jesus on the phone. So I never know what's going to happen when she answers the door, but I love it.

I knew that while not everyone would be as confident to share their faith with complete strangers, most of my family had inherited my bold and adventurous spirit.

Ruth was next to share.

I think for any child and parent's relationship, it's very hard. Children always have a challenge to see the parent as a person and I think I'm a classic example of that because it's not always easy for me to see you as a person. But I do want to tell you that what I really value about you is that you're 80 years old and your entire life you've grown and you've changed. As things have come your way, you're always growing and I think that's a really beautiful thing.

I was touched by these words. I had been through many challenges in life and it wasn't always easy to be flexible and adjust to circumstances, but God had given me grace to keep changing and growing. Although it had been challenging for me, too, as my children had become adults and chosen so many different paths, I was so thankful for them all.

Alfred's brother Herald had come from Kamloops, BC. He said,

When I think of Edna and Al they always expressed their faith. They went as missionaries and they always had devotions with their children. If there ever was a family that learned the ABC of the Gospel, those children did, because Edna and Al were very faithful in implementing the Gospel and showing a real spiritual concern for their children. And so I'm sure that Edna still prays for you all and prays that God's will be done in your lives.

Alfred and I had started the tradition of daily devotions together and, as Herald said, I continue to pray for my whole family every morning.

Grace, who had welcomed all of us into her home so many times, spoke about hospitality.

I want to thank my Mom for some of the 'genes' that you passed on to me. Besides my youthful complexion — thanks Mom! — you taught me that there is a big difference between entertainment and hospitality; Entertainment focuses on MY ability to create a wonderfully orchestrated social event, while hospitality focuses on how to make OTHERS feel welcome in my home and to provide a meal with whatever food is on hand. You told many stories of how my grandma was hospitable in her farm community. It seemed that grandma's was the place to go and 'hang out' — sew horse blankets, play cards, drink moonshine. I believe that hospitality is a generational gift and I hope it will continue to flourish in my family for many generations!

For several years, Mom and Dad lived in our basement suite in Vancouver. Our children loved to wander downstairs and see if Grandpa had any candy for them. I jokingly scolded him and said he had to pay the dentist's bills too! However, the most memorable part of my parents living with us was that I saw how much they valued praying together. They prayed daily for their children and grandchildren, for blessings and salvation. When Dad passed away Mom said that the weight of responsibility to pray for the family was heavy and more difficult than she anticipated. Thank you so much for your prayers for my family. Today, on your birthday, I want to honor you and ask that we might be able to pray for you, bless you and encourage you for the next season of your life. My heart is full of thanks for who you are.

Fern, who was teaching ESL in Washington, shared next.

I want to tell something I think is pretty representative of Mom. She loves to haggle and bargain and get a deal. I remember once in India on the way back from church - we never bought anything on Sunday - but there was a man by the side of the road selling strawberries. Mom could not resist and she stopped the car. Say he was asking five rupees or something – she offered one rupee. Then he came down, and he came down – she wouldn't move. He finally came all the way down to one. But she didn't buy it then, because it was Sunday. It was just a game.

So I've kind of gone the other way and I always pay more than they ask. Then I phone Mom and tell her and she's just so mad at me. I'll go to a garage sale and they'll ask five dollars and I'll say, 'I think it's worth seven.' So I give them seven then I phone Mom.

Everyone laughed, knowing how true this difference was between our natures.

Mark shared next. He had always had such a lively sense of humour and, although he has no kids of his own, has always connected especially well as an uncle. He said,

One time when we went to the store you gave me a penny to put in the parking meter. Then you went in the store, but I really wanted that penny. You were in the store and then I saw the parking meter lady come by, look and give us a ticket. You came back from the store and you were so mad because you had to go to the court and you had to pay the fine.

Joe was sitting beside me and I was eager to hear what he had to say.

It's nice to be here and you know why I'm here. It's been interesting being married to this woman.

Everyone laughed and he continued,

She has really delighted my life and broadened it. She's brought many joys to my life and to have somebody at this age to love me has been wonderful.

I was blessed by how he'd been welcomed into the family and was so grateful to be with him.

After everyone had shared, it was my turn. It was hard to know just what to say to sum up my feelings for all the beautiful people gathered around me. I'd watched them grow up and change and had prayed for them all so often. I began,

I really want to thank every one of you for coming, for putting forth the effort, the time and money to come here to help me celebrate my 80th birthday. This is the only time I'm going to have an 80th birthday. It's really very special and I feel so blessed and humbled to look around and see my quiver so full. God said children are a blessing from Him and that my quiver would be full. All of you are arrows in the quiver. I think there are 44 here now but God keeps adding more arrows. Arrows are for protection and security and you're all straight-shooting arrows, ready to overcome difficulties. When one of us hurts, I believe we all hurt and we are there for each other. You've certainly been there for me.

I thought about the struggles we'd faced as a family and how we had helped each other through some of the most difficult times in our lives.

You're all so very important and when I see the creativity and uniqueness — every one of you are different, those who have been added, the spouses, the grandchildren - I'm just so proud to be your mother, your grandmother, your great-grandmother. And for all the future ones that God is going to add, other spouses and other grandchildren — Mark . . .
I said, turning to my youngest son as everyone laughed.

One of the reasons why our quiver is so big is because God said to Adam, 'replenish the earth' and because our name is Adam, Grandpa felt he should do his part. I wish he was here to see you all, but he's there to welcome you all in Heaven. I'm just so proud that God has blessed me

with all these arrows - all of you special people. You're so unique and so creative.

I looked at my husband where he sat beside me.

I just thank God for Joe, someone special in my life, a gift from God. And I just want to thank you for welcoming him, because he feels at home and you've opened your heart and your homes to us. I especially want to thank Kathie and Dan for making all of this happen. Kathie has worked so hard and they've been just so generous in welcoming us into the suite downstairs. We're so comfortable and we're just so blessed to be in this home. There's such peace here that I know that the blessings are going to flow and you're going to make a difference in Ladysmith. They're here for the family and I'm just so thankful that their part in the family is so important.

As I looked around at all the different faces and thought of how each person contributed to our family, I continued:

Our family would not be complete without any of you. We need each one of you and each one of you is important to me and I love you and you're important to each other. So continue to bless each other and support each other. Every morning Joe and I pray for you and our prayer is that you will make right choices in favor of God so that the blessings can pass down from generation to generation, even to a thousand generations and so you won't need to suffer the consequences of wrong decisions. That's our prayer and I want to bless you tonight and thank you for putting this party together. It's been overwhelming and I'm really just so full of appreciation. I have a hard time expressing love and words fail me, but I thank you all for coming to be a part of this great celebration. Thank you.

On Sunday we had a big barbecue and open house and many friends from the island came to help us celebrate. It was a great weekend and just before everyone left we took a family picture on the steps of Hawley Place B&B.

From top to bottom and left to right: 1ˢᵗ row: Daniel, Mark, Grayson, Grace, David, Josiah, Eunice, Tom, Grace, Billy, Jim.
2ⁿᵈ row: Julia, Rob. **3ʳᵈ row:** Liz, Sam, Paul, Ruth. **4ᵗʰ row:** Laryssa, Fern, Laura, Allegra, Craig. **5ᵗʰ Row:** Kathie, Elsie, Eliana, Jeremy. **6ᵗʰ row:** Steve, Julian, Kalina, Tim, Liz. **7ᵗʰ row:** Jon, Herald, Jordan, Myrtle, Bruce, Melissa, Joshua, Fiona. **8ᵗʰ row:** Trevor, Myself and Joe.

Myrtle Lake August 1996

At Fern & Ray's Farm, Spokane WA September 2009

Chapter 16
Return to the Dream

My mind wandered back to the funeral and to the sound of Moira, our teacher friend from India, speaking.

My name is Moira Jackson and I was Tim Adam's teacher at Lushington Boys School in Ooty, South India in 1963/-64. I became very much a part of the Adam household. "May I sing you a special hymn that always reminds me of precious times of spiritual blessing we had at Farley, the WEC guest house in Ooty?

And Moira sang these words,

"My heart has no desire to stay, where doubts arise and fears dismay.
Though some may dwell where these abound,
My constant aim is higher ground."

Al and Edna had such a concern for the young staff at the school and paid a great cost for sharing their testimony of the infilling of the Holy Spirit with four of us "girls" from the school. But as we too sought the Lord, what a blessing we were brought into. What precious times we had in prayer and praise and sharing the good things of the Word of God on Thursday and Sunday evenings.

Thank you, Edna (and Al) for your love and your faithfulness in caring for our spiritual wellbeing. It was just thrilling that we met up again in Canada and I am so privileged to be able to come to Edna's memorial to share this part of her story.

It was nice to hear Moira confirm my memories.

My granddaughter Fiona was the last to speak. What she said touched me deeply.

Grandma's enthusiasm, dedication, and faith. These three things have always been valuable to me. Grandma was always so excited about having so many grandchildren. She always introduced me as her oldest grandchild, with pride. Her enthusiasm for life made her eternally youthful and bouncy. Her love of meeting new people, going to new places and trying new things created a very positive impression on me during my formative years.

When I was a teenager, Grandma introduced me to the world, in a way. She wanted me to experience YWAM and encouraged me to get out there and meet young people, participate in youth groups, go on trips and just generally enjoy life. I guess she could see that I was a sensitive teen, prone to depression and rebellion and so she gave me a lot of encouragement to try new things, to get out there and meet people.

Our family didn't have a lot of money, so Grandma helped to create opportunities for me, her oldest grandchild, to experience things that cost a bit of cash. One summer we went to a YWAM youth retreat in the Okanagan. I brought my cousin Ruthanna (from my dad's side of the family), and my grandma brought a nice, shy woman in her early twenties. I was sixteen. We had such a great time. I remember stopping along the way to buy peaches and cherries, and eating them in the car. We stained our clothes with sweet dark cherry juice and got sticky hands from the juice, which dripped from the succulent peaches. It was so hot and we were so sticky that we had to make an impromptu stop at a rushing river to dip in and splash around in the water. On the trip Grandma kept the conversation fun and upbeat. Even that car adventure before the retreat filled me with a joy of being alive, young, and free in the summer. I didn't feel like I had to act differently around her like I did around my other grandparents. I went home very happy.

My grandma was so good at relating to young people, and I always felt so comfortable with her. She asked me questions about my life and I never felt judged by her. She always believed that the young people, the next generation, would bring something good into the world. So when tragedy hit our family a few times with the grandchildren, I know it hit Grandma hard.

I always appreciated the way Grandma dealt with difficult situations. She always was able to express her heart, and bring humility to the situation. I learned about Christian community through those two qualities of vulnerability and humility. I know she was always devoted to pray for me and sometimes when I was experiencing difficulty, I would think about her praying for me and that would give me courage.

There are stories about Grandma's life which I've always been amazed by. She was a rebellious youth, tough and reckless, as she has said. It seems she has learned some tough lessons in life and come to cherish the basics deeply as a result-- family, love and God.

I used to brag about my Grandma when I was younger. I would tell people how many countries she had been to, or that she was self-taught in a lot of ways. I always thought of her as an interesting and dynamic person, open to life, and feeling every moment of it. I think I even said that I wanted to be like my grandma on more than one occasion. And I still do. I want to have enthusiasm, dedication and faith that grow with age. I love you, Grandma!

In my dream at the funeral I heard a trumpet playing, "When the Roll is called up Yonder I'll Be There."

I had one last Divine Appointment to attend. An angel escorted me to the gates of Heaven. There at the gate stood my Jesus, full of glory and grace. "Well done," he said to me.

Alfred was also there, holding out his arms to welcome me. I was so happy to see him. I also wanted to see my mansion, the one I'd seen in a dream many years ago. In that dream, it was built on a hilltop with a road leading up to it. The outside wasn't elaborate, but the inside was striking. In the living room the carpet was fascinating, its colours and pattern like nothing I'd ever seen. They flowed across the floor and blended up into the drapes. There were no lamps because in Heaven, Jesus is the light. The bedroom had a four-poster bed and unique furniture. In the living room was a table with bevelled edges, the centre covered in velvet. All around it were high back, carved wooden chairs. In my dream everything was perfect and one-of-a-kind, the colors just for me. The Decorator knew me better than I knew myself. I knew that it was ready and waiting for me to move in. An angel guided me to my mansion and I couldn't believe my eyes; it was even more elaborate than in my dream. I took possession immediately.

After I was settled in, Alfred showed me around Heaven. Everywhere we went there were mountains, rivers, lakes and sandy beaches. The streets were paved with gold. My mind went wild with ideas for the next family reunion. I couldn't wait to see everyone again face-to-face and show them my mansion. I prayed they would all be there. We would wait for their arrival to welcome them with open arms . . .

Edna's Family History

John (Johann) & Matilda Feuerbach Family
Parents

- John (Feuerbach) Fierbach DOB: March 1876 Death January 21, 1968, age of 92 yrs.
- Matilda (Schoenfeld) Feuerbach DOB January 30, 1881 Death May 8, 1943, age of 62 yrs.

Children 12

- Arthur Feuerbach and William Feuerbach born and died as children in Volhlynia.
- Emma (Feuerbach) Frederick DOB July 30, 1902 Death June 7, 1966, age of 64 yrs. Married to George Frederick DOB Dec. 22, 1897 Death Dec. 16, 1988, age of 91 yrs.
- Helen (Lena) (Feuerbach) Wensel DOB Oct. 15, 1904 Death Feb. 14,1976, age of 72 yrs. Married Sept. 6, 1920 to Julius Wensel DOB Sept. 29, 1888 Death July 11, 1979, age of 91 yrs.
- Manuel (Mac) Fierbach DOB January 14, 1906 Death Feb. 28, 1978, age of 72 yrs. Married Dec. 26, 1936 to Annalisa Freida (Winter Fierbach) DOB April 22, 1916 Death Nov. 16, 2002 age of 86 yrs.
- Roy Fierbach DOB Dec. 14, 1907 Death Sept. 12, 1956 age of 49 yrs.
- Henry Fierbach DOB Feb. 26, 1911 Death July 16, 1977 age of 66 yrs. Married April 22, 1939 to Evelina (Evelyn) (Baker) Fierbach DOB Jan. 22, 1921 Death Oct.25, 2000 age of 79yrs.
- Leo Fierbach DOB Jan.1, 1913 Death Feb. 21, 2001 age of 88 yrs.
- Edward Rudolph Fierbach DOB Jan. 28, 1915, Death Sept. 8, 2003, age of 88yrs.Married May 1, 1941 to Elma(Semler) Fierbach DOB April13, 1918
- Leonard Fierbach DOB Aug.13, 1916, Death March 23, 1997Married June 27, 1964 to Mary (Lauender) DOB Death
- Elsie (Fierbach) Rapke DOB Dec. 1, 1922 Married July 4, 1942 to Lenard Rapke DOB Sept.27, 1913 Death March2, 1993 age of 80yrs.
- **Edna (Ernestina) (Fierbach) Adam, Simpson** DOB Oct. 6, 1924 Married Aug 19, 1950 to Alfred Adam DOB June 18, 1924 Death Nov. 16, 1988 age of 64 yrs. 2nd Marriage to Joe Simpson DOB March 3, 1929

Children 7

- o Fern Louise (Adam), Henderson, Conne DOB July 28, 1951 Married June 9, 1973 to Lee Henderson divorced June 1999 Married September 5, 1999 to Raymond Edward Conne DOB December 12, 1950

Children 4
- o Fiona Mary (Henderson) Marion DOB March 24, 1974
- o Brady Andrew Henderson DOB December 1, 1975
- o Ian Daniel Henderson DOB June 25, 1977 Married August 18, 2002 Brenda Rene (Santamaria) Henderson DOB June 12, 2002

  Children 2
  - ▪ Owen Carlos Henderson DOB March 2, 2003
  - ▪ Celeste Reyna Fern Henderson DOB January 4, 2009
- o Donall Reid Henderson DOB February 4, 1982

o Daniel Alfred Adam DOB December 20, 1952 Married May 5th 1978 to Kathleen (Mason) Adam DOB December 27, 1958
Children 2
- o Joshua Daniel Adam DOB August 25, 1979
- o Jesika Pearl (Adam) Reimer DOB January 21, 1981 Married April 6, 2002 to Mathew Reimer DOB May 10, 1980

o Grace May (Adam) Bain DOB May 27, 1954 Married July 15, 1978 to Grayson William Bain DOB December 6, 1953
Children 4
- o Samuel Ian Bain DOB December 5, 1979 Married May 7, 2005 to Elizabeth Sally (McCormick) Bain DOB
  Children 1
  - ▪ Autumn Joy DOB July 5, 2010
- o Stephen Andrew Bain DOB December 10, 1981
- o Paul Alfred Bain DOB April 22, 1985
- o Laura Ruth Bain DOB September 3, 1987

o Timothy John Adam DOB April 13, 1956 Common Law Marriage 1987 to Laryssa Markiana Wolanski DOB October 27, 1952
Children 2
- o Julian Daniel Adam Wolanski DOB June 3, 1987
- o Allegra Yohanna Wolanski DOB May 10, 1982

o Ruth Esther Adam DOB December 31,1957 Married April 30, 1977 to Bruce William Campbell DOB February 2, 1995
Children 4
- o David Alistair Adam Campbell DOB October 28, 1979, Death May 13, 2008 Married July 31, 2001 to Marcie Estelle Rae Randall DOB November 13, 1979 Divorced
  Children 2
  - ▪ Estelle Ruth Campbell DOB October 7, 2001
  - ▪ Laurel Rae Campbell DOB November 17, 2003
- o Robert Simon Adam Campbell DOB June 29, 1981 Married August 13, 2003 to Julia Marianne (Slofatra) Campbell DOB December 21, 1981

Children 2
- Sienna Grace Campbell DOB April 7, 2009
- Kate Frances Campbell DOB June 19, 2010
  - Heather (Grace) Adam Campbell DOB November 16, 1983
  - Jordan Michael Adam Campbell DOB April 21, 1988
- Eunice Joy (Adam) Snell DOB April 25, 1962 Married April 27, 1985 to Tom Charles Snell DOB February 1, 1958
Children 6
  - Jeremy David Snell DOB June 12, 1986
  - Elizabeth Anne Snell DOB June 12, 1996
  - Jonathan Alfred Snell DOB April 12, 1989
  - Josiah Jay Snell DOB August 17, 1992
  - Eliana Joy Snell DOB May 31, 1995
  - Kalina Margaret Snell DOB June 6, 1998
- Mark David Adam DOB October 10, 1967 Partnered September 2008 to Silvia Graber DOB November 23, 1971

Fern, Daniel, Ruth, Timothy, Me, Eunice, Mark and Grace
I am very proud of all my children and thank God for blessing me.

My Quiver Full of Grandchildren and Great Grandchildren

First Row: Jonathan, Josiah, Eliana, Kalina, Jeremy, Elizabeth
Second Row: Celeste, Ian, Brenda, Owen, Fiona, Donall, Brady
Third Row: Laurel, David, Estelle, Jordan, Grace, Julia, Kate, Robert, Sienna, Julian, Allegra
Fourth Row: Samuel, Autumn, Elizabeth, Paul, Laura, Stephen, Joshua, Jesika, Matthew

Book Review

By Sharon Nault

This story is a "WOW". First of all, the funeral format is just right. It is so unusual it will catch the reader in its grip and hold them. Just the beginning is going to inspire readers to think about their own lives. It makes them subtly uncomfortable enough to draw them in. The way you handle the subject of death is inspired and you give the reader the right perspective on it. It's a lesson in a story.

Too old, too old for what? That phrase has stuck with me since the first time I heard you say it. It is like a battle cry that rings out to older people and is just what they are looking for, what they need to hear. It is like saying to people with very few words, "Hey you out there! You can get up off the couch! You can get going! So what if you just turned 70! God has a plan for you! Go on!"

Your writing is very crisp and to the point. I like that style very much. I think the Lord may carry this book on beyond the boundary of family and friends and give it an expansive life of its own.

Ordering Information

To order a copy of this book or to contact the author Edna Adam, please use the following addresses:

Mailing Address:
Edna Adam
1500 Spa Road
Box 2073
Niland, CA 92257

E-mail Address:
joedna@msn.com